LEARNING FROM MEDJUGORJE

What is the Truth?

Fr. René Laurentin

Translated by Fr. Francis Martin
Original French:
Apparitions De Marie A Medjugorje
Où est la vérité?
Published in France by CEDAC

Learning From Medjugorje
What is the Truth?

ISBN 0 932085-05-9

The Word Among Us
PRESS
P.O. BOX 369
GAITHERSBURG, MD 20877

CONTENTS

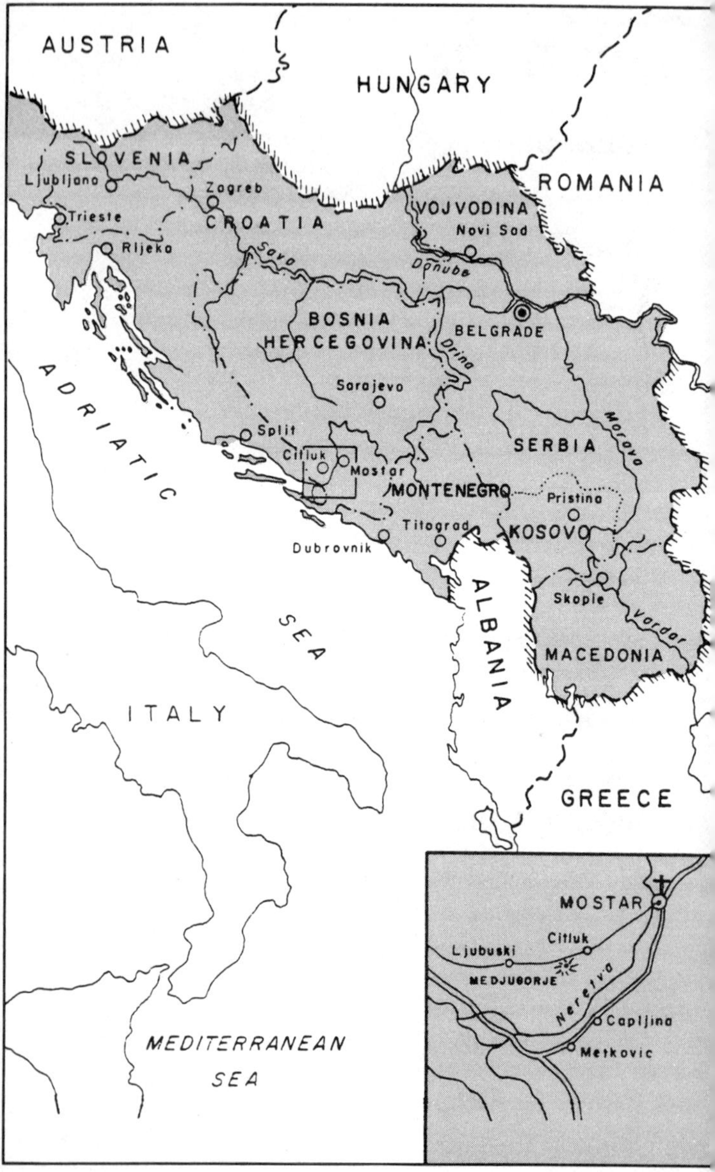
AUSTRIA
HUNGARY
ROMANIA
SLOVENIA
Ljubljana
Zagreb
Trieste
CROATIA
Rijeka
VOJVODINA
Novi Sad
Sava
Danube
BOSNIA
HERCEGOVINA
BELGRADE
Drina
Sarajevo
ADRIATIC
Split
Citluk
Mostar
SERBIA
Morava
MONTENEGRO
Pristina
Titograd
KOSOVO
Dubrovnik
ALBANIA
Skopje
Vardar
SEA
MACEDONIA
ITALY
GREECE
MEDITERRANEAN
SEA
MOSTAR
Citluk
Ljubuski
MEDJUGORJE
Neretva
Capljina
Metkovic

FOREWORD

THIS WOMAN IS 2,000 YEARS OLD

The Gospa appears to us." For seven years now, six young villagers of Medjugorje have been saying this. In Croatian, "the Gospa" means "the Madonna." At Lourdes, in 1858, the name was "Notre Dame," "Our Lady."

That there are "visionaries" who claim to see an invisible person goes against all common sense. This "foolishness" has elicited derision from the worldly-wise and calumnies from those who say it is not so. The Catholic news media of both right and left, despite their conflicting ideologies, are often joined in opposition to the apparitions. This crystal-clear message of the Virgin Mary inviting people to pray, fast, and seek peace and reconciliation surprises and disturbs some people. Yet day by day, it succeeds in convincing and changing many honest doubters who are happy to find Life once again.

If Our Lady is visiting our world, as these young people say, that is really good news. But it is the kind of news that cuts across the wisdom of the sophisticated. If you find yourself among the latter, then do not read this book. It is written in keeping with the simplicity of those most principally involved in the event.

These young people, who are like other folk, "neither better nor worse than others" as they say themselves, attest to the truth of what they claim by the whole of their lives. Both the human and spiritual qualities of their lives are constantly being demonstrated, to surprising depths in the cases of some of them who are precisely the most simple and natural among them and the best-equipped to deal with difficult situations in communication. While remaining calm, without losing touch with reality, these young peasants were astonished from the outset.

"Now I will never be afraid to die," said little Jakov on the very first day.

What overwhelms them is not so much the beauty of the apparitions as the love that is there, direct, simple, and intimate. "After a thousand apparitions, I would be tired of them," said a young theologian from Zagreb. "So would I," answered Vicka, "if it weren't for love. You don't get tired of loving."

In the same vein, little Jelena, who has the grace of seeing Our Lady "in her heart," asked her one day, "Why are you so beautiful?" "Because I love! Love,and you, too, will be beautiful."

Mary's familiarity is that of a sister and a mother. Her unimaginably deep relationship to the Son of God, the Creator of the world, has transformed rather than deformed her, and has not made her complicated. And so, this young woman of twenty centuries ago finds herself on common ground with the young villagers. She has more in common with their naiveté than with our speculations about a God who may be only "a meaning" or than the net result of our language. She cuts through the film of language for them. And the "meaning" becomes obvious for them in these meetings. Some theological approaches asphyxiate the faith; but among the young people at Medjugorje, faith breathes.

Foreword

The eternal young woman whom these youngsters claim to see is two thousand years old, according to our calculations. In 1984, Jelena was given to understand that Mary's birthday is August 5th. On that day, the two thousandth anniversary of Mary's birth was fervently celebrated with a day of prayer, preceded by three days of fasting. This was done without detracting from the liturgical feast of Our Lady's nativity, duly observed on September 8th.

Actually, Our Lady is outside of time. The today of her glory does not dim the yesterday of her humble life here on earth with Jesus Christ. In the eternal youth of God, she still remains the young Jewish girl of yesteryear who lived a difficult life, yet one full of adventure in the despised town of Nazareth in Galilee. She well knew the exhausting work of a woman of those days. There was no running water; one had to go draw water from the well and carry it back along the road. There was no electric oven; one had to go gather wood. No matches; one had to keep a fire going all day. There were no bakeries; one had to grind the grain, knead the dough and bake the bread. There were no ready-made clothes; one had to spin the thread, weave the cloth, and make the clothes.

Mary gave birth to the Son of God, the Savior of the world, by the unheard-of miracle of a virgin birth. Why this seeming folly? Not out of any contempt for marriage, because this was a special birth. According to the wonderful plan of God, every new human person is born of the love of two other human persons, and this itself is a great mystery. But the person to whom Mary gave humble birth here on earth was already existing. He was a divine pre-existent Person. He had forever been Son of God before becoming son of Mary and part of the human race. This was not the birth of a new being but the manifestation of He who IS. As the Protestant theologian Karl Barth boldly said with great insight: to signify this mystery, some other sign was required than that of sexuality (of male arrogance). That is why Mary, totally taken hold of by God and totally given over to him, from the earliest moments of her life, resolved in her heart to belong to God alone, to "not know man" (Luke 1:34). This resolve prepared her for her mission.

She, thus, gave birth in the poverty of a manger to the Divine Son, who was destined for the most terrible and painful of deaths. Mary's mission was to give to God what He did not have: weakness, humility, and an ability to suffer and die. These he shared with her. This humble woman was needed to give to God a vulnerable solidarity with us so that through it, He could save us.

This mystery of love was accomplished by following a path of joy, sorrow, and glory. At the end of this path, neither Jesus nor Mary remained disinterested in our lot.

That is why Mary cannot stand it any more. Seeing men slide toward self-destruction on the comfortable slope of sin, she comes to visit her people who are in danger of death. She comes to put an end to the disaster of her children who calmly give themselves over to their own ruin. The last picture which the Bible gives us of her is this: in the heavens, a woman clothed with the sun and crowned with twelve stars (there are in fact twelve stars in the Medjugorje vision). Mary is returning to visit the earth wearing the raiments of that description. The light of the Son of justice precedes, surrounds, and follows this apparition.

- In 1531, in Guadalupe, Mexico, she appeared not in the colony of the conquerors but among the oppressed

Indians. Thus was born the indigenous Church of the New World.

- In 1830, she came to Rue du Bac, to set a Church wounded by the revolution back on its feet again. In 1858, at Lourdes, she came to rekindle the gospel among the poor, in flat contradiction to the iron law of the 19th century: "Get rich."

- In 1917, at Fatima, she came urgently to the aid of a world about to destroy itself. This modern world believed that it had found its freedom by proclaiming the death of God and the miracle of progress. But instead, it gave birth to the First World War and the spiritual death of man.

- Now after the Second World War, in a world which is inexorably preparing for another and more apocalyptic war by an unprecedented stockpiling of arms, Medjugorje repeats the message of Fatima. It is a pure message, free of political calculation, and both the Pope and those responsible for the shrine at Fatima and the parish at Medjugorje have consistently kept it so. Both messages foresee the conversion of Russia.

The poet wrote: "I have written this story simply, simply, simply, to the rage of the wise, wise, wise, to fascinate little, little, little children." This could well apply to the story that God is writing in the hearts of simple people in Medjugorje.

Jesus said, "If you do not become like one of these little ones, you will not enter the kingdom of heaven."

It Happened in Yugoslavia

The Medjugorje apparitions are taking place under a regime that is professedly atheist. It is, however, the most open country in the Marxist bloc; it is Mediterranean, thus humane. It is an independent country, the only one to have established diplomatic relations with the Holy See. There is a Yugoslavian embassy in Rome and a papal nunciature in Belgrade. It encourages tourism, thus attesting to the fact that it does not lie behind the famous "Iron Curtain" that we hear so much about but, rather, has friendly borders. Facing Italy, the dazzling Dalmatian coast presents itself for all the world to admire.

This country is a kaleidoscopic federation, more complex and more explosive than Lebanon:

- 5 nationalities: Serbian, Croatian, Slovenian, Macedonian, and Montenegran. In 1960, the regime added the "moslem nationality" to cover the Croat followers of Islam. There are also 18 ethnic minorities.
- 6 republics
- 14 languages
- 2 alphabets
- but only one party: Communist

From the religious point of view:

- 14 million Orthodox
- 6 million Catholics
- 2 million Moslems
- plus some Protestants, Jews, and other religions.

Despite smoldering tensions that are more serious and complex than those of Lebanon, this Balkan country remains admirably welcoming and peaceful.

This is the only country in Eastern Europe where apparitions could occur without violent oppression but rather under a subtle control somewhat baffling to foreigners. The youngsters were interviewed several times by the police, and were subjected to medical and psychiatric tests (June 27 and 29, 1981), but they were not imprisoned. Furthermore, at the insistence of their parents, who had the courage to appeal to the law, the interrogations ceased. By law, such interrogations could be made only in the presence of the parents. The imprisonment of the pastor and a few others was stopped. The legal harassment to which I was subjected has also ended.

In 1985, first the Slovenian television and then the national television (on October 17) provided very objective coverage of these apparitions. They were a real testimony. One can only pay tribute to the professional talent and the objectivity of those newsmen.

While the apparitions were initially viewed as a Croatian "clerical-nationalist" political plot under the aegis of Our Lady, this interpretation has been completely reversed by the patience and openness of all those involved. Today, the Yugoslav press proclaims: "These apparitions are a purely religious phenomenon, hence legal and beneficial to the nation's economy."

How Many Apparitions?

Often some very fanciful numbers are produced, but even these have to be provisional since they increase by at least one every day.

As of the date of the 5th anniversary (June 24, 1986), the daily apparitions had been going on for 1,825 days. However, the young people told Fr. Tomislav Vlašič sometime before March 1982 that there had been five days without apparitions. This would drop the total to 1,820, since there were no subsequent days without apparitions.

On the other hand, there have been frequent occurrences of several apparitions on the same day. For instance, on February 24, Marija and Ivanka saw the Virgin twice. Then on February 17, the Gospa disappeared and reappeared. Are we to count this as an interrupted apparition or as two? Finally, Marija and Ivan often have a second apparition during the evening vigils of their prayer group on the mountain (about twice a week).

Furthermore, there were six youngsters at the outset seeing apparitions. Today, there are only four. If, as some people do, we multiply the apparitions by the number of youngsters, we have another variable component.

Then there is the question of Jelena's interior visions. Should these be taken into account? There are as well those occasions when the youngsters see the apparitions separately (as has normally been the case for Vicka since 1984). Should these be considered together or separately? Integrating these variables with these criteria and accounting for various aspects of unknown factors would be a complex task even for a computer.

The only dependable count is the number of days. At this moment, that total is over 2,500.

CHAPTER ONE

A BRIEF HISTORY OF THE APPARITIONS

First Phase: On the Hill.

Wednesday, June 24, 1981
First Day: At the Foot of the Hill.

The apparitions at Medjugorje began on June 24, 1981, in the afternoon, in the hamlet of Bijakovići, one of the four hamlets that make up the village of Medjugorje.

Two young girls, Ivanka, 15 years old, and Mirjana, 16 years old, were taking a walk at the foot of the hill. They were villagers on vacation in Bijakovići, where their families have a house. The sky was overcast. Ivanka had just lost her mother two months earlier. She already had a serious suitor whom she dreamed of marrying soon. School no longer interested her.

As they were returning, they reached an intersection in the small road just at the entrance of the village. Ivanka looked up and saw, some 250 yards up on the hill, a bright silhouette on a small cloud. She whispered, "It's the Gospa."

Mirjana was more practical. She was soon to begin her studies in Sarajevo in agricultural engineering. She did not even look up. "That can't be the Gospa," she said.

Whereupon both of them became frightened and raced

into the village as fast as they could. People made fun of them. However, something drew Ivanka and Mirjana, and they went back that same afternoon about 6:30 p.m. along with Milka, a shepherdess who, at 14, was the youngest of the Pavlović children. "Come help me bring in my sheep," Milka asked them.

The sheep were grazing some 600 yards from the village along the road of the apparition. It is called "Podbrdo" because it runs along the foot of the hill. On their way out of the village, the three girls saw nothing. On the way back, however, near a small tree about 120 yards from the intersection, Ivanka once again saw something and the others did, too. The sheep, meanwhile, found their own way back to the fold.

Just then, Vicka came along. She was 16 years old, and the neighbor and constant companion of Ivanka and Mirjana during vacation time. All three had agreed to go for the walk just completed, but Vicka had been called to Mostar to make up a math examination. Worn out by the stress, the exam, and the bus ride, she took a nap and missed the walk. The others waved to her: "Vicka, look up there…the Gospa."

Vicka was both attracted and annoyed. She took off her sandals and ran away from there as fast as she could. On the way, she met two friends, Ivan Dragicević, 16 years old, and Ivan Ivanković, 20 years old. They went back to rejoin the three young girls, who could still see the bright silhouette up above. They had hardly arrived when the first Ivan, thoroughly frightened, ran away by jumping over a fence, losing his bag of apples in the process. The second Ivan was troubled and did not stay.

This apparition was not forcing its way in. No one was

coming to it without some reflex of defensiveness.

Vicka overcame her reaction. She stayed there and looked at the far-off silhouette. It was a woman. She seemed to be holding a child, cradling him in her right arm. She motioned to them to come closer, but none of the four girls dared to do so.

When they got back to the village, everybody made fun of them. "You saw flying saucers!" As a result, Ivan Ivanković, the eldest of the six at 20 years of age, would not go back the next day.

The rustic open area of Bijakovići, lying between the green fields of grapevines and tobacco and the rocky hill against which its houses were built, was awakened to a mystery.

Thursday, June 25
Second Day: Up There, So Close.

"If it is the Gospa, maybe she will come back," the youngsters said to one another.

Marija, sister of Milka, the shepherdess, joked about it along with everyone else. But she told Vicka, her friend, "If you see anything, come get me."

So the three inseparable companions, Ivanka, Mirjana and Vicka, went off. There once again was the Gospa, crowned with sparkling stars, shining with light on the cloud on which she stood. That day, they were not afraid of her. Rather they were drawn to her "as though they had never met so much love."

But then Vicka, faithful to her promise, ran off to find Marija. Milka, her little sister, wanted to tag along but her mother stopped her. "You have work to do. Marija can go." Marija, the cook, had time before dinner. She left the stove which had not yet been lit. Little Jakov Čolo, 10 years old, who was there, went along with them.

As soon as they were together, they climbed the hill with amazing speed. There they found Ivan, who had come up another way with some of his friends. It was the attraction of the apparition that brought them together. For the first time, he and the five who came up from Podbrdo saw Our Lady up close: loving and simple, really indescribable. Her shining robe was silver gray: her black hair was wavy under a white veil. The twelve stars in her crown were held in place by nothing and were not connected to each other. Her blue eyes looked at them with affection.

Ivanka got up the courage to ask her, "Where is my mother?" "She is happy; she is with me." Her voice was soft, "like music," "like bells ringing."

Mirjana said to her, "Give us some sign; otherwise, they will think we are crazy."

Those blue eyes radiant with love definitely united this group of young people. One could not have imagined a more disparate group: boys and girls, of different ages, ranging from a total extrovert (Vicka) to a deep introvert (Ivan). This gaze, this prayer, welded them together for a common mission: Ivanka and Mirjana, Vicka (the oldest girl, to be 17 the next month), Marija, and the two boys, Ivan Dragicević, 16, and Jakov, 10, the only child among these older adolescents. Everything was against them. There were the external pressures which continued to increase, from family, church, and police, and there was the fact of the deep differences of temperament, age, etc., among them. But Our Lady brought them together in one movement and common mission, in a journey made easy by love. Their daily meetings with her deepened their unity among themselves despite all that ought to have divided them day by day, external forces and internal differences. It seemed to them that the Virgin liked nothing more than to see them all together before her. This was possible only during vacations; the reopening of school split them up.

Friday, June 26
Third Day: Faith and Reconciliation.

On the third day, again at 6:15 in the evening, an exceptional light drew a veritable crowd, two to three thousand people, to the hill. The young people were waiting down at the foot of the hill where they had seen the apparition the first day. They were accompanied by a mechanic named Marinko, a neighbor, who offered to guide them on the hill.

Our Lady signaled to them. They went up the hill with incredible speed. The only guide they needed was the apparition which drew them.

Vicka, as Bernadette once before her, had brought along some holy water to test the authenticity of the apparition. "If you are Our Lady, stay with us. If not, leave us!" Mary only smiled through this dousing with holy water which Vicka continued energetically until she emptied the whole bottle.

"Why have you come here and what do you want of us?" asked Ivanka. "Because there are some strong believers here. Also, so that you might be converted and make peace among the people."

Medjugorje was a divided village. There had been some people wounded and even three killed just before the war on the very spot where the church now stands, on the boundary between Bijakovići (the hamlet where the young people came from) and Medjugorje (the principal hamlet). The Gospa added, "I have come to convert and reconcile the whole world."

A neighbor suggested, "Ask her to give us a sign of her presence." "Blessed are those who have not seen and believed!" answered the Gospa.

Mirjana asked her, "What is your name?" "I am the Blessed Virgin Mary."

Then she repeated earnestly the key word of the message, "Peace, Peace, Peace! Be reconciled." Peace and reconciliation, these are the basic words of the message.

Saturday, June 27
Fourth Day: Believe Like "Those Who See."

On June 27, the police took the young people to Čitluk to be questioned and to undergo psychiatric testing. Dr. Ante Vujević declared them to be of sound mind. They left hurriedly so that they could arrive on the hill by 6:30 (all but Ivan).

At the request of two Franciscans who were present at the apparition, Vicka asked Our Lady, "What do you expect of priests?" "That they be strong in their faith and that they help you."

"Why don't you appear to all the people? To the Church?" "Blessed are those who believe without having seen."

She disappeared. They prayed. She reappeared, greeted by their hymn, "You Are All Beautiful."

Vicka asked insistently, "Our Lady, what do you expect of these people?" On the third repetition of the question, the Gospa answered, "That those who do not see believe just as those who do see."

Marinko, who had been helping and protecting the young people, hard-pressed by the crowd, asked to be shown the exact spot of the apparition and then indicated the place with a stone marked with a white cross.

Sunday, June 28
Fifth Day: 10,000 People on the Hill.

The pastor, Fr. Jozo Zovko, returned from a preaching mission some distance away near Zagreb. He had just arrived home the day before to find an incredible effervescence in this parish which he considered sleepy. He questioned the young people; he took advice. His preaching recommended prudence: "The Church is stern in these matters. We have to avoid being overhasty. Let us not go along with these young people blindly."

That evening about 6:00, somewhere between ten and fifteen thousand people jammed the hill. A tape recorder was playing. The young people, during the apparition, transmitted Our Lady's answers to the questions that they posed:

"That the people believe and persevere in their faith."

"That the priests be strong in their faith and help you."

"Blessed are those who believe without having seen."

After an interruption of the apparition, "That those who do not see believe, just like those who do see."

Then their heads and gazes turned upward. She had disappeared, going up. "Ode! She has gone," whispered one of the youngsters. "Her light has disappeared." She said,

"Go in the peace of God."

Two Franciscans, dressed in secular clothes, went along to witness the event. This was against the advice of the pastor, Fr. Jozo Zovko, who had called for the recitation of the rosary at the church in order to divert the people from the hill. He had a crowd as well.

Monday, June 29
Sixth Day: The Morgue and More Psychiatry.

On Monday, the 29th, the police once again brought the young people for a psychiatric examination, this time to the hospital at Mostar (the principal town and the seat of the diocese). They had to wait in the hallway. On one side, the insane were walking around in a courtyard; on the other side was the morgue, open, with its corpses. This made quite an impression on Mirjana, but Vicka said jauntily, "We know well enough that we all are going to die!"

Dr. Duda confirmed their psychological balance. Upon returning for the apparition, they received this message: "There is but one God, one faith. Believe with strength, with confidence."

There was a three-year-old child there. Weakly, his little head rested on his father's shoulder. He had been suffering from septicemia virtually from birth. His parents pleaded. The youngsters interceded. The Virgin encouraged prayer for his healing. "He will get better." During that summer, he came back walking and talking. This was the first in a series of improvements in health or cures which has continued to multiply. As of October 19, 1986, the church rectory registered 291 such cures. By 1987, the number was over 300.

The Second Phase: Banned from the Hill

Tuesday, June 30
Seventh Day: Far Away, in Cerno.

On Tuesday, the 30th, the crowd waited in vain for the young people. Early in the afternoon, two young women, Ljubica and Mirjana, who had been contacted by the police, took the young people for a ride to get them away from the hill where the large crowds were a source of concern for the police. In Sarajevo, they suspected a clerical-nationalist plot. The young people were tired, worn out by this new experience, which gave a whole new dimension to their lives, and by the constant questioning. They accepted the diversion happily. The seven of them were all crammed in the car, the two young women and five of the youngsters. Ivan had refused to go. They visited the falls at Kravica (Yugoslavia's little Niagara). Then they went on to Čapljina where the two young women offered them cake and fruit juice.

At the usual time of the apparition, they were still on the road between Ljubuski and Čitluk. On the right, little Jakov could make out on the horizon the blue of the hill. He insisted that the car stop at the entrance to a pathway. Then he ran along the path until the point where it began to slope downward.

There a light arose over the hill on the blue horizon. The Gospa was coming toward them, very close on her cloud. "Would you be angry if we waited for you at the church?" asked Mirjana. The police had forbidden them access to the hill and had threatened their families.

The Gospa seemed to hesitate: "Yes, at the usual time."

Back at the parish, the pastor questioned them for a long time at the rectory, recording the proceedings on tape. Ljubica and Mirjana were there as well, uneasy because they also had seen the lights. They were soon to give up their assignment from the police.

Wednesday, July 1
Eighth Day: The Apparition in the Van.

On the next day, July 1st, during the afternoon, just before the usual time of the apparition, the police staged a raid on Bijakovići. Three girls, Ivanka, Mirjana and Vicka, were loaded into the police van. But suddenly the van disappeared as far as they were concerned: there was only the apparition, unexpected and short.

Thursday, July 2
Ninth Day: The First Apparition at the Rectory.

Tension was beginning to rise at Bijakovići. The police had their eyes on the comings and goings of the young people. They felt hunted. Marija's sister, Ruica, went to consult Fr. Jozo: "What are we going to do?"

Upon returning, she created a diversion and then had the young people taken by car to the rectory. There, they had the apparition in the third room on the left as you enter. They were alone because the pastor had gone to the church, already filled by the crowd well ahead of the scheduled mass at 6:00 p.m.

The youngsters attended as well. There was a great deal of fervor. Fr. Jozo Zovko had been talking about restoring bread and water fasts for some occasions. Up to this point, he had been preaching in a desert, to third-order

Franciscans only. He now proposed a fast of bread and water for three days in order to obtain light on this matter.

The crowd of enthusiastic parishioners responded: "We want to do it." Before dismissing the people at the end of mass, Fr. Zovko invited Vicka and Jakov to speak. The tape of their remarks is still preserved.

"And now a little boy is going to talk to you; you can't see him because he's too small." His head did not appear above the altar, but his voice was firm: "Today, I asked Our Lady to give us a sign. She only nodded her head, like this [affirmatively] and then she disappeared. Before she left she said, 'Good-bye, my angels." ' This is a loving term in Croatian, which grandmothers use when talking to their grandchildren.

Friday, July 3
Tenth Day: Go Out and Protect the Youngsters.

That Friday, the pastor, Jozo Zovko, prayed in the church and asked for light: "Lord, you spoke to Abraham and Moses. I carry the weight of all these people. Enlighten me!"

"Suddenly," as he tells it, "I heard a voice which said to me: 'Go out and protect the youngsters.' I left my Bible and breviary, genuflected and opened the door. My hand was still on the doorknob when I saw the young people running toward me: 'The police are after us. Hide us!' They were crying. Ana, an older sister of Vicka's, was with them.... I led them into the rectory to an unoccupied room [the third on the left]. Then I left the rectory and locked the door."

He went to the church just as the police were coming

out: "Have you seen those youngsters?" Like St. Martin when he met his persecutors, he pointed in the direction from which they had come: "Yes, that way." The police took off in hot pursuit.

While this was going on, the room in the rectory was transformed for the young people. Our Lady was there, very joyful in contrast to their fear. She comforted them and they prayed and sang with her: "Do not be afraid; you will have the strength to bear everything!"

Saturday, July 4
Eleventh Day: Everyone at Home.

Saturday, the 4th of July, was a day of uncertainty and confusion. After all the threats, interrogations, and medical examinations, the young people, overcome by these events, thought that the apparition of Friday, the 3rd, was the last one.

Then, on that day, Our Lady surprised them, appearing to each one where they were. The apparitions were not finished at all. So they began to ask again: "Where should we meet tomorrow?"

The Pastor Becomes a Visionary.

Every day then, about 6:00 p.m., according to circumstances, in the home of this person or that, in the fields or in the rectory, Our Lady appeared to them. Sometimes, the apparitions took place in the church during the liturgy.

Fr. Jozo Zovko, who was accountable to these people, to the Bishop, to the police, and to God himself, was still perplexed. However, one day in church toward the end of the rosary, he saw the apparition along with the young people at the same spot next to the pulpit.

Suddenly, his preaching from the Bible which heretofore had been studious and tedious, became powerful and full of fire. The police who liked the low-keyed style of his earlier sermons began to worry.

Jozo Is Arrested

Fr. Jozo's sermons remained beyond reproach. However, by August 12th, the pressure was mounting. The police had dug out of his July 11th sermon, which had been duly recorded, something for which they could indict him: "He said, 'Forty years in the wasteland!' " It had been just forty years since Tito had come to power. Thus, this man said the revolution was a wasteland! The sermon was subversive!

On the 17th of August, the police descended on the rectory. They sequestered the sisters, confiscated the collection, and arrested the pastor.

A long trial began. The lawyer defended Fr. Jozo's use of "forty years in the wasteland." He was speaking of the Hebrews led by Moses on their journey to the Promised Land more than three thousand years ago, as told in the Bible. But then other charges were found in order to justify the trial. On October 22nd, Fr. Zovko was condemned to three-and-a-half years in prison. He was freed after a year-and-a-half, thanks to the forty thousand letters written to the President of the Republic by the readers of the weekly, *Sabato*.

Right after the arrest, Fr. Tomislav Vlasić hurried to the rectory, now leaderless. He evaluated the difficult situation and left for Mostar where he reported to his Franciscan provincial, Fr. Jozo Pejić. With admirable foresight, the provincial responded: "You take over. I am naming you the pastor of Medjugorje."

Tomislav thus became the spiritual guide these youngsters and the parish needed.

Third Phase: The Chapel of the Apparitions

(February 1982 - April 1985)

After January 1982, the apparitions took place more and more regularly in the small room opposite the sacristy which had formerly been used as a storeroom. It thus became "the chapel of the apparitions" and is revered as such even to this day. It is there that the Gospa appeared until the end of March 1985, the date when the Bishop issued his prohibition: "The young people may have visions wherever they choose, at home or elsewhere, but not in the church buildings."

This raised a serious problem of conscience for Fr. Tomislav Vlasić. To leave the youngsters to themselves meant to leave them vulnerable to the importunities of the crowds, especially the less stable among them. It also meant exposing them to the police since any religious demonstration outside of a church constituted a misdemeanor. This would have meant a reversion to the situation of the early days, which had been precisely so smoothly resolved by transferring the apparitions to the church with the tacit approval of the police.

Fourth Phase: At the Rectory Since April 1985.

It was Archbishop Franić who came up with the solution: "Why not allow apparitions in the rectory?" That is where they have taken place ever since.

The apparitions continue to be a formation for the young people as well as a catalyst for the prayers of the pilgrims.

The pilgrims accept, for better or worse, this dissociation between the apparitions and the liturgy, whereas previously the two were integrated in harmony. Between the rosary and the mass, Our Lady's discreet visit would lead the praying congregation into the Eucharistic celebration along with the young people who would pray for a while with the crowd. In such a situation, one can almost hear her words, referring to her Son, "Do whatever he tells you" (John 2:5).

Where is this Leading?

Since the apparitions began, the youngsters have received a series of secrets having to do with the future salvation of the world and the threats weighing upon it today. Mirjana was the first to receive the tenth and last secret. This was at Christmastime 1982. It was accompanied by this announcement: "You will not see me any more except on the day of your birthday and when important circumstances require it. You will go back to living by faith alone like everybody else."

This was very hard for her. "I thought I would get very depressed," she told me at Sarajevo on March 24, 1984. But through prayer, she adjusted quickly to living the night of faith. Her life was difficult at that time. Always under the watchful eye of the police, an object of suspicion at her school, living in the secularized, even atheistic, world of Sarajevo, she was also experiencing family difficulties. For nearly two years, she lost contact with Medjugorje and there was concern that she was backsliding. But she persevered in prayer, discreetly, adapting to her difficult life.

Beginning on August 26, 1984, Mirjana has experienced nearly every month new apparitions or locutions (interior words). This is to prepare for the public revelation of the ten secrets which will mark the end of the apparitions. She has chosen the priest who is to make them known. He is Fr. Pero Ljubičić, the youngest of the three Franciscan priests of the parish.

On May 6, 1985, Ivanka, the only one with Mirjana at the first apparition, June 24, 1981, received in her turn the tenth secret. Our Lady promised her an apparition every year, not on her birthday as was the case for Mirjana, but on the 25th of June, the anniversary of the first apparition. (June 24th was really more in the nature of a first contact from a distance, but the group of six had not yet been constituted.)

On June 25, 1986, Ivanka spent a long time in prayer, preparing for the promised apparition, but she was not anxious. The apparition occurred at home at the usual time. After an absence of 14 months, she saw the Gospa for 14 minutes. Our Lady recited two prayers with her: the "Our Father" and the "Glory Be." This dialogue with the Gospa ended the long period of waiting in her engagement to Branko. It was no doubt after having submitted her own free choice to Our Lady that she married Branko the following January 6 (1987).

What will happen now?

For more than three years now, Mirjana has been preparing for the final outcome which she continues to say is near. As of this writing, the revelation of the secrets has not yet begun. Why? The substance of Mirjana's answer to me was: "It is a merciful postponement."

In other words, prayer and fasting have offset or slowed down the self-destruction to which the world's sin is driving it, for the majority of the messages are concerned with imminent dangers which only a return to God can temper.

The young people keep guard over the secrets closely, though they speak about the general meaning and direction of what they have heard. When the secrets are to be revealed, this is the procedure that must be followed:

- Ten days before each secret, Mirjana will notify Fr. Pero, who is responsible for revealing them.
- He must fast for seven days and then has the task of revealing the secrets three days before they are to take place. He remains the judge of his mission and could keep the secret for himself as John XXIII buried the secret of Fatima, whose revelation had been authorized for 1960. However, Fr. Pero's firm intention is to make the secrets known.

The first three secrets are three final warnings to be given to the world as a last chance for conversion. The third secret, which is also the third warning, will be a visible sign given on the hill of the apparitions to convert those who do not believe.

Then will come the revelation of the seven last secrets, which are weightier. This is particularly true of the last four. Vicka wept when she received the ninth secret and Mirjana did the same upon receiving the tenth. The seventh secret has been mitigated because of the fervor of the prayers and the fasting.

These prospects remain puzzling. Secrets are always fascinating, but generally lose their authority once they are revealed. We saw this in the case of Fatima. Besides, predictions of the future are subject to optical illusion. The early Christians thought the end of the world was near, and the apostle Paul himself thought he would see it during his lifetime (1 Thessalonians 4:13-17). Expectations, fed by hope and prophecy, foreshortened the events. Finally, this detailed scenario with which we are presented at Medjugorje could appear to some to be more like magic than a revelation of God's mysteries.

Will there be disappointments when the ten secrets are revealed? Is their delay already a premonitory signal? These are good questions. The prudence and vigilance which the Church recommends apply in a particular way right here.

Faith is certain. God himself infallibly guarantees it. The charisms are fallible. They are the gifts of God wrapped in human frailty.

I have no doubt at all concerning the authenticity of the grace conferred at Medjugorje, on the young people who see the apparitions, on the parish, and on the hundreds of thousands of pilgrims who have experienced a deep conversion. But this does not guarantee every detail of the predictions and premonitions concerning which the young people have already made mistakes as, of course, did some saints, even canonized saints. It would be possible to miss the point by becoming polarized by the secrets and the "sign" which has been talked about. Then one would fail to see the grace that is growing with such an inner consistency and depth that it is far superior to any externals.

A Brief History Of The Apparitions

CHAPTER TWO

THE APPARITIONS: GENUINE OR COUNTERFEIT?

What should we think of these apparitions whose influence has been so widely felt? There is a good deal of discussion about this.

At first, the Bishop was in favor of them, even enthusiastic; that was until August 1981. After that point, he began to swing toward the other side for reasons that were mostly concerned with local affairs. He was embroiled in an inextricable conflict with the Franciscans. Founders of the faith and practically the only priests in the diocese for four centuries, the Franciscans still make up about 80% of the clergy. The secular clergy, reestablished since 1881, would like to regain seven other parishes, but the parishioners who are deeply attached to the Franciscans are obstructing this move with that vigor characteristic of Croatia. The apparitions are taking place in a Franciscan parish. Some Franciscans who have been having difficulty with the Bishop have been assiduous with regard to Medjugorje. They asked that the Gospa be consulted, and the question was put to her thirteen times. The answers reflect the different temperaments of each of the different youngsters. Bishop Žanić seized on the hardest answers and thus arrived at this conviction to which he constantly reduces the whole problem: "This Virgin is against the bishop; therefore, it is not the Blessed Virgin." From that point on, he has gone back and forth between various and quite different explanations which have in common that they are negative. Thus, the apparitions are due to: the manipulations of the Franciscans, parapsychology, some unknown causes, hallucination, make-believe, "pantomime," or even diabolical phenomena.

Nevertheless, a number of very qualified people have recognized the clarity and spiritual fruits of these apparitions. Among bishops, there are the Archbishops of Split and Pescara. Among theologians and other leading churchmen: Fr. Hans Urs von Balthasar, Fr. Michael Scanlan (President of the University of Steubenville in the United States), and the late prominent Pentecostal, David DuPlessis. (See: R. Laurentin, *Is the Virgin Mary Appearing at Medjugorje?*, Gaithersburg, MD: The Word Among Us Press, 1984, pp. 135-136.)

What is the Pope's view? He is following what is happening with interest. He has read my books as well as the reports of the French and Italian doctors, and he has transmitted these to the appropriate Congregation in Rome. He tries not to involve himself in this specific matter which concerns the leaders of the local church, and this is in keeping with the tradition of the Holy See to act according to the principle of subsidiarity. While there may be some indications of where his sympathy lies and while it is true that he did receive a pilgrimage from the parish of Medjugorje and sang the pilgrimage hymn with them, we should not try to second-guess him or ascribe to the Pope a particular judgment. The Pope has deliberately avoided expressing any judgment so as not to influence personally the investigation that is going on.

One thing is clear at least: the Holy See has blocked the negative judgment which the Bishop of Mostar had announced would be delivered in May 1986. When the Bishop went to Rome in April 1986 to submit his findings, Cardinal Ratzinger, Prefect of the Sacred Congregation for the Doctrine of the Faith, asked him to suspend judgment, to put everything in the hands of Rome, and to dissolve his commission. Bishop Žanić did this with exemplary obedience on May 2, 1986. Thus, the local diocesan commission whose majority was opposed to the authenticity of the apparitions of Medjugorje (9 to 4) never completed its work.

Responsibility for rendering a judgment about the apparitions was transferred to the Yugoslav Bishops Conference. The judgment will no doubt be a long time in coming, and this for two reasons:

1. It is difficult to render a judgment so long as the apparitions have not come to an end. The best of things can turn sour in this world of sin.

2. It may be impossible to form a commission within the framework of the Bishops Conference. The two key members who would have to play a fundamental role are: Bishop Žanić of Mostar, within whose diocese Medjugorje is found, and who is violently opposed to the apparitions; and Archbishop Franić of Split, the President of the Doctrinal Commission of the Bishops Conference. He is so favorably disposed that he has often said: "The apparitions have done more for the faith of our people than all of our pastoral care over the past 40 years."

The mutual opposition of these two is too strong to allow for any real cooperation to develop between them. This means that there is no way of beginning new proceedings which could shed new light on the apparitions. Hence, we will just have to await a verdict.

Does that mean that we must abstain or remain disinterested parties until then? No, not if it is really a matter of an urgent message from Our Lady. When someone cries out, "Fire!" or "Robbery!" healthy prudence dictates that action, not waiting, is called for. The *official* judgment will have to wait. Discernment need not wait any more than at Lourdes where the prayers of the crowds at the grotto and the healings began among God's people long before the Bishop rendered his judgment. Without anticipating the official judgment, we should wait with respect and obedience. It is important to see clearly in matters such as these. That is why, in keeping with the tradition and spirit of the Church, which I have come to appreciate deeply during thirty years of study, I have investigated and published so much regarding Medjugorje, mobilizing the collaboration of many sciences in the service of the Church.

Let me confide to you that all of this has been for me a revelation of a very particular sort. For nearly 30 years, I have been studying about apparitions in dusty archives, in the austerity of historical study. But, now, I have had direct contact with visionaries and their ecstasies. I had described Bernadette's ecstasy but without really understanding what I was writing, depending on the eyewitnesses of that period. Today, as I reread that description, I finally understand it. I grasp now how Bernadette's voice could disappear without her realizing it when she was speaking to the apparition. Our tests at Medjugorje show locution without phonation. I understand how being disconnected from the world of one's immediate surroundings facilitates the perception of another world, and how this can happen with perfectly normal people. I understand how being unable to receive impressions from without during an ecstasy helps to shield someone from the vicissitudes of this world.

An objective assessment should weigh the reasons for and against. On the advice of Bishop Žanić, I began with such an assessment in my basic book, *Is the Virgin Mary Appearing at Medjugorje?* I will not spend much time on such an enterprise here since it seems to me that, with varying degrees of success, I have answered the objections in that prior book.

One of the most frequent objections is the long duration of these apparitions, more than seven years now. "That proves they are false," a Bishop told me recently in Lourdes. No doubt he was trying to test me. It is true that apparitions in modern times have been quite brief (only one at La Salette and Pontmain, 18 at Lourdes). However, certain mystics in the Middle Ages and in the 17th century and even in our own time (with Padre Pio) were the recipients of apparitions and other spiritual communications during their whole life.

There are many reasons which can explain the long duration of these apparitions. It takes time for a message to travel in an Eastern country where communication is limited. Then, too, it takes time for a message to travel in our repetitive and materialistic world where daily television drowns out spiritual impulses. Especially, it takes time for formative teaching, at a deep level, to bring about changes in the prayer groups, the parish itself, and the pilgrims who are drawn to the place. It is the time required for a mother to teach her children. This is one of the essential characteristics of Medjugorje.

Then, too, difficulties of various kinds, first with the Church, then with the Bishop, may have made prolonged support necessary. Finally, the serious situation that was tempered by prayer and fasting resulted in a merciful postponement, according to the reply Mirjana once made to this question.

Briefly, these problems and others are amenable to solutions which can be more or less complete, even though certain questions may still be unanswered and even though the youngsters themselves may not have been free from error in every detail. We have the example of Ivan when he reacted to the authoritarian pressure of the episcopal commission to make him reveal his secret. Similarly, Vicka asked for and transmitted ardent oracles in favor of the two Franciscans in trouble with the bishop: "You only think of those two," the Gospa told her humorously.

For the sake of brevity, I will limit my comments to four reasons why we should take these apparitions seriously, respecting the criteria of the Church:

- What is taught with regard to faith and morals;
- The consistent and non-pathological nature of the ecstasies;
- The healings and other signs which take place there;
- The spiritual fruit developing from the apparitions.

Faith and Morals

In the eyes of the Church, these are the foundational criteria. Are these apparitions in conformity with faith and morals? Archbishop Franić, who was a member of the

Doctrinal Commission at the Vatican Council (in which I participated as an expert) and is now President of the Yugoslav Doctrinal Commission, considers the apparitions to be beyond reproach. He went so far as to state: "I do not see what objection could be brought against them."

The diocesan episcopal commission (today dissolved) and certain opponents thought they had found some objections, but the points they raised were not very serious and are answerable. They remind one of the arguments of the judges of the Sorbonne who declared Joan of Arc to be a heretic and a backslider. Anyone who reads the proceedings that led to her being burned at the stake can easily grasp on whose side lay the faith and the understanding of the faith. It was in the lucid clarity that Joan possessed and not in the erudite quibblings of her judges whose science is outdated today.

The Ecstasies are Authentic

1. The evidence of the medical tests.

What struck me immediately was the simplicity, the naturalness, and the open quality of the ecstasies. There was nothing tense or distorted; there was nothing rigid in any way about the youngsters in their minds or their bodies. However, it was necessary to verify these first impressions on medical and scientific grounds and, in that regard, I had the good fortune to find collaborators of the greatest competence. Two groups of doctors studied the ecstasies.

The French team was headed by Professor Henri Joyeux of the University of Montpelier, winner of the International Prize for cancer research. (See: *Scientific and Medical Studies on the Apparitions at Medjugorje*, Dublin:

Veritas, 1987.) The Italian team was coordinated by Drs. L. Frigerio and G. Mattalia along with a team of ten specialists. (See: *Dossier scientifique sur Medjugorje*, being translated, to be published by the same editor as above.)

Briefly put, the conclusions, supported by many video cassettes, are as follows:

- The seers in ecstasy are not in a pathological state.
- They do not sleep or dream during the apparitions.

This is established by electroencephalograms conducted on several of the youngsters. This test explores the activities of eight significant areas of the brain. It shows, for instance, how a driver falls asleep at the wheel of his car during a long drive. In an auto equipped with dual controls, the brain activity of the driver is recorded and the curve reveals this phenomenon very clearly. At the beginning of the trip, one notes the pulsations of a normally awakened state: a mixture of alpha impulses (receptive, for the driver is looking at the road) and beta impulses (reactive, driving requires foresight). When the driver becomes sleepy, sleep impulses start to take over; these are soon crossed by dream flourishes.

In regard to the young people, it is different. Before the ecstasy, there is a mixture of alpha impulses (10 cycles per second) and beta impulses (20 cycles per second). The receptive/reactive ratio is about the same as for a driver in his or her normal state. When the ecstasy begins, the beta impulses stop. Everything is in the rhythm of pure alpha impulses: the state of monks in prayer. This is a state of being *awake*, not one of being asleep or dreaming. The electroencephalogram also ruled out epilepsy. This test combined with clinical observation also ruled out pathological hallucination.

The young people at first refused to be tested. They did not want to be guinea pigs. When Our Lady was asked about further tests, after the experiments of Dr. Botta (March 25, 1984), she replied: "It is not necessary."

2. Neither hallucination nor pathological state.

We finally managed to convince the young people by saying: "It is not necessary for you and it must not interfere with the essential which is prayer. However, it is necessary for those who do not believe, starting with the Bishop who has repeatedly said that these are collective hallucinations. We cannot ignore the possibility of checking on his hypothesis which has been considered authoritative until now."

Because our tests ruled out hallucination, I so notified the Bishop in June 1984. He, however, continued to maintain his position until the time he issued his Report of October 30, 1984, which he disseminated to the prinicpal episcopal conferences of the world and the world press, concluding:

> Proceeding in a responsible manner, the Bishop of Mostar after mature reflection has arrived at the conclusion that it is morally certain that the events at Medjugorje are a case of collective hallucination.

Once again, I conveyed to him my astonishment and he conceded my point in an honest way. He wrote to me personally in January 1985 that he was withdrawing his hypothesis of hallucination and inclined rather toward the notion that all this was simulated. However, our tests equally ruled out this hypothesis. There can be no question of hysteria, epilepsy, hallucination, or catalepsy. (Professor Joyeux in *Scientific and Medical Studies on the Apparitions at Medjugorje*, Dublin: Veritas Publications, 1987 pp. 53-54, 74-75.)

3. The youngsters' state is coherent and functional.

The ecstasy is a state which is healthy, coherent, and functional.

The young people are disconnected from the external world. They do not perceive the objects around them, neither sound nor color. This disconnection facilitates the perception of an object of a different order: the apparition.

Similarly, the fact that their voices are not heard when they speak with the apparition protects the intimacy of their dialogue.

During the ecstasy, their insensitivity to pain (scientifically established by Professor Santini) helps to take them away from the events of this world. However, their bodies retain their normal suppleness and perform the necessary reactions to regain their position when, for example, someone pushes them or raises them from their kneeling position. Through all of this, they are completely relaxed. Their state of being unaware of all of this helps them enter into another state, open to perceptions of a deeper sort.

Completely normal in their daily life, they are no less so during the ecstasy. Is their happiness which transforms them something that comes from beyond?

4. Visions or apparitions?

Are these perceptions subjective or objective, that is, are they visions or apparitions? This is a question frequently asked. The dilemma is clear enough, but it presents the problem poorly. It is beside the point since all knowledge implies both a *subjective aspect* and an *objective aspect*. These two aspects are not contrary or mutually exclusive: they are rather correlative.

The subjective aspect is, in a way, the reverse side of objective knowledge. All human knowing has a subjective aspect for two reasons:

1. It is an act of the subject, the person knowing.
2. The subject is affected by the impact made by the object.

Some sound vibrations reach my ear and activate my nervous system. The impact is subjective, but it is this impact which is the condition for my objective knowledge. If I see colors, it is because light waves, which have no color but varying frequencies strike my eyes. This impact is transmitted by nerve impulses. They form a current similar to electricity, which travels by means of a physical-chemical process that is also uncolored. The brain deciphers the stimuli which reach it and, therefore, modify the knowing subject. By these complex methods, the subject makes a direct connection with the object, let us say a tree which a person clearly perceives as being definitely outside himself and at a certain distance.

Subjective impacts are the means of objective sense knowledge, which no one doubts during his whole life except in cases of mental illness. "I saw it. I heard it," we say and generally no one takes exception. What is subjective does not exclude what is objective, rather it conditions it. The activity of the subject in the act of knowing attains to its object by means of exterior signals which impinge upon the senses. These are the ABC's of any correct understanding of knowledge which is characterized by intentionality, that is, by the capacity to perceive another precisely as other.

In investigating the functioning of sense perception, some philosophers used to say: "Perception is really an hallucination. There is neither color nor sound, but only vibrations and other nerve impulses that stimulate visual and auricular illusion."

I used to be impressed with this conclusion but, now, I see that it is a false reading of the evidence. An hallucination is a perception when there is no object, whereas the perception of color is certainly the perception of an object. Little by little, I have come to understand that vibrations and nerve impulses are the means to knowledge. They are, as it were, the two sides of it. There is a functional correlation between the front and the back, the front side and the underside, in many domains.

The artisans who produce the marvelous Gobelin tapestries work on the *underside* where they can conveniently knot all the threads. However, the truth of the tapestry is not on the underside but on the front side; it is there that we see the final result. In the same way, the final product of the organs of sense is to allow us to know, in a true way, the external world in its visual and sound dimensions. In this way, pleasure and beauty are joined to objectivity.

The perception that the young people have *is not produced by the ordinary means of sense knowledge*. This was established several times by a test using a screen as early as January 1982. Fr. Kustić, the editor-in-chief of *Glas Koncila*, asked the young people to close their eyes during the apparition. This did nothing to affect the vision. Similarly, Dr. Stopar put himself between Marija and the vision. Afterwards, he said triumphantly: "Today you saw nothing. I was between you and her." Marija answered, "Oh, that's why I saw her today as though through a slight fog." For her, the corpulent doctor had been but "a slight fog." The same thing happened when Dr. Phillippot of our French medical team interposed a screen which he did on several occasions.

It is quite clear that if the perceptions took place by ordinary means, all those in the room would see the apparition. Should the fact that the perceptions are not ordinary force us to conclude according to the outlook of idealistic philosophy that the apparitions are completely subjective?

This conclusion is in no way indicated. The perceptions of the visionaries contain many criteria by which objectivity can be established:

I. Young people testify: "We see the Virgin like a real person with three dimensions. We can touch her. We have touched her."

II. When they look at the apparition, all their eyes converge on the same point. The normality of their ecstasy ought to caution us against an overhasty suspicion of their witness. The inner coherence of their lives confirms their testimony.

III. The reactions of the six young people to the apparitions occur with a synchronic rhythm that gives every sign of objectivity.

If there were only one of them, it might be easy to label this rather exceptional vision as purely subjective. But when six young people see the same thing at the same time in a similar way, it is difficult to maintain such a conclusion. How can the synchrony of their common experience be explained? What sort of pre-set arrangements could they have made that would lead to such a unified reaction? No one has yet been able to come up with an answer. Initially, we thought maybe it could be done by a signal of some sort, but no signal could be detected. Quite the contrary, everything confirms the absence of a signal. Furthermore, no signal could explain the number and variety of their unified reactions.

The six most obvious examples of synchrony are the following:

1. *The young people kneel at the same time*, the only variance being each person's rhythm of reaction.

2. Their voices disappear at the same moment, as they are in the act of kneeling. This synchrony is difficult to measure, but it is remarkable nonetheless.

3. *The voices are heard again at the same moment* to continue the prayer: "...who art in heaven, hallowed be Thy name." In the early days, people used to ask them, "Why do you skip the first two words of the 'Our Father'?" They answered, "Because it's the Virgin who says, 'Our Father,' and we pick it up from there."

Here, again, the synchrony varies with the reaction time of each youngster, but on several occasions there was perfect simultaneity.

4. After the recitation of the "Our Father" and the "Glory Be" (no "Hail Mary" because they are praying with the Blessed Virgin), *the voices disappear again, simultaneously*.

5. At the end of the apparition, *all eyes are raised at the same time*. To those who seem surprised, the youngsters explain, "The Virgin rises and disappears."

6. Finally, one or several of the youngsters exclaims with greater or less synchrony, *"Ode!"* (which means, "Gone!").

"Watch carefully to see if the 'Ode!' precedes the raising of the eyes," Professor Cadilhac told Mrs. Joyeux, who was conducting the methodical investigation of the synchronies. "That could be the signal."

There was no ambiguity in her findings. In every apparition, the raising of the heads and eyes occurs *first*. Then when this movement has reached its apex, the "Ode!" marks the disappearance.

To these six synchronies, two others may be added of which the young people are totally unaware, but which were revealed by the electro-oculograms. This test performed simultaneously on Ivan and Marija on December 28, 1984 showed that before the apparition, the eyeballs are mobile, as they normally are, for our eyes move and vibrate to observe the world around us. However:

7.From the moment the ecstasy begins, the eyeballs become immobile and cease exploring the external world. (*Scientific and Medical Studies*, pp. 65-66.)

8.At the end of the ecstasy, the eyeball movements begin again, with a disparity between the youngsters of about one-fifth of a second.

To summarize, the ecstasy is a non-pathological state. It is a healthy, coherent, and functional state as in all authentic knowing. The knowledge gained in the ecstasy, which is of a unique type, is received by the subject in accordance with subjective impressions which we do not have the means to identify. However, this knowledge should be fundamentally classified as objective. The ecstasies at Medjugorje conform to the traditional experience of Christian mysticism.

All the synchronies just studied eliminate the possibility of pure subjectivity. The only simple and coherent explanation is the one given by the youngsters themselves. They see, objectively, a real person. Meeting her deeply satisfies them and educates them spiritually in a remarkable way, though to varying degrees. Everyone can see and admire that in each of the young people.

Admittedly, we are dealing with a complex process. It confronts our ignorance because we know so little about it. Basically, we are in touch only with the receiver, the young people, and not the sender, the Virgin, whom they say they see. That presence does not belong to our world of space and time within which she manifests herself only to the young people. It is not brought about by ordinary material means, by vibrations whose specific frequency reaches the eye or the ear. Vibrations may stimulate the optic and auditory nerves, but the subjects do not perceive them. Similarly, if we are gripped by some show on television, we do not notice the cat walking around.

IV. Our tests also eliminated the possibility of dream or hallucination. We are dealing then with a communication which, though less material, is no less real. The youngsters experience it as more than real. It is immediate, direct, existential. It is a person-to-person communication between the young people and Her whom they recognize as the Virgin Mary. It is a concrete, intensely personal perception brought about in a spiritual manner, but which is embodied in the visual center of perception according to means which are beyond our probing.

This communication is vastly different from what a perception of a spaceship coming from another planet might be. For the distance between these young people and Our Lady is not within measurable space (miles or light years). It is the more radical distance between our dimension of space/time (changing and successive) and the dimension of space eternity of which God is the measure. This explains the mysterious nature of this experience which takes the young people out of the dimension of clock time. Whether the ecstasy be long or short, they are equally satisfied. That is because they leave for a while the ordinary orbit of time in order to gravitate for a moment in that of eternity.

To sum up, the explanation which best takes account of all the data is that given by the youngsters themselves. They really and lovingly see Our Lady, who communicates with them in a way which is, in the full sense of the term, mysterious.

Let us move on now to examine other criteria of authenticity: the signs. These are the healings and other extraordinary phenomena.

The Signs

1. The healings.

Healings are being multiplied at Medjugorje. There are many of them: 291 have been reported to the rectory so far. There they are noted on forms that are well-designed and which have been complemented at times by medical certificates.

At the beginning of 1984, I submitted to Dr. Mangiapan a descriptive inventory of an early sample file. He quite correctly pointed out that these allegations had no conclusive value unless a complete file were established. Nonetheless, he added:

> The relatively high number of (alleged) healings can be seen as paralleling what Dr. de Saint Maclou used to call, when Lourdes first began, the miracle of numbers.

> Nine reports seem to merit a more detailed investigation: four cases of infant sickness; tumor cases, particularly one among them; finally, cases of kidney infection treated by dialysis.
>
> Nine cases worthy of study out of fifty-eight alleged. A good score, I wrote, to the author [R. Laurentin], if they can be authenticated by a more objective analysis.

By 1987, the total number of healings was no longer 58 but 291, of which about 10 seem worthy of further study.

The episcopal commission of Mostar never undertook a real study of the hearings. The Bishop, intent on arriving at a negative verdict, devoted his attention to seeking out who had died among the sick for whom healings had been hoped, prayed, and thought to have been received at Medjugorje. In his Report dated October 30, 1984, he mentioned only the four deaths he had managed to uncover, particularly that of a sick person whose operation failed despite the prayers of the young people. But these deaths prove nothing. Even those who are miraculously healed finally die. What is important in cases like this is to examine those who are healed contrary to all expectations, and who are thanking God for it. That is what Dr. Stopar did. And in a particular way, this is what the Italian doctors, all members of the Regina Pacis Association (a group founded for the defense of life), did.

Among the healings now under study, the most remarkable and thoroughly studied is that of Diana Basile (See: *Scientific and Medical Studies*, pp. 100-105.). Briefly, this mother of three children had been suffering since 1972 from multiple sclerosis. This had involved complete blindness in the right eye (retrobulbar optic neuritis); numerous motor problems of both upper and lower limbs that rendered her a cripple; and total urinary incontinence that caused a skin infection throughout this area.

On May 23, 1984, upon entering the chapel of the apparitions (with the aid of crutches), her whole life suddenly flashed before her eyes like a movie, while an internal warmth renewed her whole being. She was cured. The next day, she walked barefoot from her hotel in Ljubuški to Medjugorje (about 6 miles). She was not tired at all. That same day (Thursday), although she was completely unused to such things, she climbed the hill of the first apparition.

In regard to this healing, Professor Spaziante has set up an exemplary file of 150 entries, which is technically more advanced than that of the three multiple sclerosis patients recognized among the 64 miraculous cures at Lourdes. Despite the diagnostic problems multiple sclerosis poses, the cure of Diana Basile is better-documented than the other three cases just referred to. These were judiciously recognized by that earlier, highly-qualified specialist, Dr. Thiebaut.

But we should not become fixated on the verification standards that are in force today for healings. Established according to the criteria of the 18th century, improved at the beginning of this century, they are unsuitable and out of touch with the development of medicine and theology. (I seem to be repeating the same point, but nobody listens.) Dr. Mangiapan lucidly observed that the present mode of verifying miracles is heading for extinction. Increasing acts of thanksgiving occasioned by the many cures at Medjugorje prove that what is happening there continues to develop. This very development calls for an updating of anachronistic criteria adopted during the era of scientism.

This is an old story. Christ's healing of the blind man was questioned according to the criteria of that day's experts, the scribes. But the man born blind was certainly in the right when he said, as do many of the sick healed at Medjugorje: "I only know one thing. I was born blind and now I see." (John 9:25.)

It was for this reason that I allowed room for spontaneous witnesses to healings in the chronology of the book, *Medjugorje. Récit et message des apparitions*, without waiting for complete medical examinations which would be possible only in a minority of cases.

The Italian doctors have undertaken the gigantic task of checking some of the 291 healings registered by the parish of Medjugorje. May they bring about some progress in the very methods by which they study this phenomenon.

2. The phenomena of light.

Many pilgrims are surprised to find at Medjugorje some phenomena having to do with light, quite similar to the phenomena that amazed the crowd at Fatima on October 13, 1917. Witnesses of that "miracle of the sun" were able to take only a few black and white photos of mediocre quality. At Medjugorje, we are in a better position because we have more documents. In addition to several testimonies, I have assembled some color photos and especially some videocassette films. I am still looking for specialists qualified to evaluate them, though I am well aware of how difficult it is to have certitude in this matter.

I offer the following by way of provisional conclusion:

1. Against authenticity is the natural explanation of many

of the striking phenomena:

- Photos taken directly at the sun sometimes reveal beautiful starry rays adorned with multi-colored bubbles.

- If one looks directly at the sun just before it sets, after an instant of being dazzled, the whole center appears dull surrounded by a scintillating crown. Personal fervor could see this as a beautiful icon of the Eucharist: a Host surrounded by glorious light. This phenomenon, which someone had me test in Brittany, can hardly be claimed as a miracle of Medjugorje.

2. Some other facts of various kinds remain unexplained:

- There are solar phenomena at different times and of different types which are difficult to assess. The vagaries of the photoelectric cell in the presence of the sun are able to produce some remarkable effects which are not supernatural.

- More rarely, but about thirty or forty times, other phenomena have been observed near the cross of Križevac. The cross disappears and, in its place, there is seen a dull globe with a luminous column rising above it or a silhouette that reminds one of the miraculous medal. (One may consult *Scientific and Medical Studies*, p. 6 of the illustration insert after p. 90.)

While waiting for competent studies to be made in these matters, we cannot emphasize enough the need for prudence among those who could be tempted to look for such phenomena at Medjugorje. First of all, these signs in the sky are not essential; what is important are prayer and conversion. These are the best and most important miracles. Secondly, it is dangerous to stare at the sun looking for signs. To look at this blazing star and to interpret the agitated reactions of the eye as extraordinary phenomena is to tempt heaven. There have been two accidents.

The Fruits

The greatest sign of authenticity is that given by Christ Himself.

> There is no such thing as a good tree producing worthless fruit, nor yet a worthless tree producing good fruit. For each tree is known by its own fruit. (Luke 6:43-44.)

At Medjugorje, the fruit has a depth and inner coherence that is remarkable at every level.

1. The young people.

In the first place, this fruit is found in the lives of the young people who see the apparitions. Every time I visit them, I find them both more natural and supernatural; they are growing simpler and more mature in the Lord. Every day, these young peasants, simple and guileless (naive, if you take that word in its best sense), must face very difficult problems that could throw them off-balance and seem to have no solution. Yet they resolve them. They maintain their life of prayer and fasting. Three among them, in a way which is particularly evident, have arrived at a startling depth. In them, I admire the results of the formation being given by the one who appears to them. The results show the delicate influence of a real mother who is in no way possessive, but rather sets her children free, urges them forward, and affirms them both individually and collectively.

2. The parish.

The parish maintains a level of prayer and fasting that is unique in the Church. Of course, human weakness is still present and there are varying degrees of this intensity. Nevertheless, the hardcore of the parish is at a level quite similar to that of the young people themselves. Others are coming along and growing at different speeds. There has been a remarkable progress in faith, prayer, fasting, conversions, and even reconciliation (between divided villages or families, as we noted earlier). Their capacity to welcome others and show hospitality remains a stable witness of their spiritual growth. It is something unique in our century.

It has taken great pastoral wisdom to cultivate this exceptional degree of Christian life while avoiding the pitfalls and deviations which always threaten and oppose such enterprises. This same pastoral care has awakened among the most fervent in prayer a second generation of charisms. I am speaking of Jelena and Mirjana and the group around them. The messages which they receive from Our Lady are teaching them in depth. We have here something of great promise for the future of the Church.

3. The pilgrims.

There are many conversions among the pilgrims, who come from all over the world. This requires mobilizing a number of confessors unequaled anywhere else in the world. There were 70 priests hearing confessions on August 6, 1984. One of them who chanced to come on that day remarked: "I shall remember this day more than the twenty years of my life as a confessor."

This grace extends well beyond the pilgrims. This was a surprise for me. I had written *Is the Virgin Mary Appearing at Medjugorje?* with the same degree of faith as my 80 preceding books. I never heard that any of the others had occasioned any conversions. As for Medjugorje, however, I have been deluged with daily mail in which young and old from 15 to more than 80 years of age write to me: "I read your book, I began to pray again. I went to confession. I fasted...." These fruits do not come from me but from something beyond me. That is why I keep on despite dissuading factors that seem overwhelming. For at a time when there are so many sterile fig trees, fit only to be cut down, one must protect the trees that are bearing good fruit. Why is it, unfortunately, that the opposite is so often the case? Let us hope that, as Our Lord said in the parable, the sterile fig tree will be given one last chance before being cut down.

The judgment made about Medjugorje based on its fruits is decisive. What are we to think of the three adversaries of Medjugorje who wish to see there nothing but the work of the devil? The one thing that these have in common is that none of them has ever been to Medjugorje. They judge by analyzing (and distorting) some second- or third-hand texts which are often mistaken. If the devil were prompting so many conversions and confessions, if the devil were promoting prayer (including the rosary), confession, communion, fasting, and reconciliation, then the devil himself would have been converted.

The fervor which these apparitions have stirred among Christians everywhere, despite unprecedented obstacles, is itself a guarantee of their fundamental authenticity.

The future is not assured. The opposition is enormous (from both right and left) and human beings are fallible. We must pray that this movement perseveres and continues to deepen amid contradiction. I am always surprised that human errors are so rare, of such little consequence, and so well-resolved that they turn to the good of those who are being persecuted.

Medjugorje is a grace for the Church. Bishop Žanić himself, though he is opposed to the apparitions, acknowledges their fruit. However, he sees it as coming from the fervor of people mistaken as to the authenticity of the apparitions. But the fruit of which I have just spoken is not the transitory result of misguided fervor.

And What About You?

Why have the apparitions at Medjugorje had such spiritual repercussions? This is due to the amazing power of grace in this place of faith. This grace has come at the right time. The way in which theology and Church administration are out of touch with reality in our age has left many Christians in a state of suffocation, further aggravated by the cultural criticism, suspicion, and agnosticism so characteristic of these latter years. Faith has lost contact with God. It has become bogged down in reductive ideological interpretations which have lowered faith to the level of the sciences of this world, even though these sciences are not aware of it. The Creator appears as some distant, mythical, unreal hypothesis, the uncertain result of a language whose meaning is endlessly argued.

Medjugorje brings back concrete and unmistakable signs like those of the Bible. Here, once again, the living presence of God is evident.

Many people have written telling me of the joy of rediscovering this evidence. God does exist. Christ and the Virgin are actual, living, real persons, not myths. They are interested in us. We have not been reduced to having a monologue on a phone whose wires have been cut.

This gift of God is offered to you freely. You are not obliged to believe in Medjugorje. The Church is quite liberal when it comes to apparitions. In the best of cases, she takes time before recognizing them. While waiting (and this usually takes several years), she allows the faithful to be the first to discern these signs from heaven. Their radar (*sensus fidelium*, as they say in Latin) has always out-distanced the verdict of the authorities. Sometimes, the verdict has not even been rendered since it has become superfluous. There has never been an official judgment of the apparitions that took place at the Rue du Bac, though Pope John Paul II visited the chapel there.

It is normal that Christians look for signs from God. When you love someone, you wait for him and rejoice at his coming. Of course, we have to avoid illusions, contempt for others, illuminism, and haste. The Church is alert to these matters and invites us to prudence. This vigilance is remarkable at Medjugorje despite the unusual fervor and enthusiasm, for there is a shadowy borderline where contact with God is made in mystery.

When the authority of the Church examines apparitions, it is for the sake of those who believe. If the people did not believe, the Church would not have to bother. The Church intervenes to verify whether or not this belief is well-founded. She leaves a great deal of freedom. Even when the Church recognizes an apparition, she does not oblige people to believe. The Church says only: "You may believe. It is good to believe. But if you don't believe, it is not a sin." If a Christian does not believe in Lourdes or Fatima, this is not a matter for confession. In brief, the apparitions are freely placed at the service of faith, which is free in so many regards.

The magisterium of the Church teaches the Creed. To whoever rejects the Creed, the Church says in the name of God: "You are pronouncing your own condemnation because you are denying God and the truth of His revelation." When it is merely a question of discerning the authenticity of an apparition or a miracle, be this at Lourdes or Fatima, the Church is restrained. You are free.

However, if grace has touched and beckoned you, if grace seems to be in that place, what should you do? First of all, be grateful. A visit from someone whom we love is always good news, especially when he seemed to be far away or to have disappeared. The visit of Our Lady at Medjugorje is like that. "I thought you were dead," we often say to someone dear to us who had given us no news or "sign of life" for a long time.

The good news of this visit is all the more welcome because our world is in such a serious condition. We are nearing the second millennium, a time full of dangers and promises. By her messages, Our Lady is shedding light on this exciting but dangerous road. She is showing us how to address our uncertainty and confusion. Blessed are those who find out in time what they must do to further the best and oppose the worst.

This is the message of Medjugorje. It has no other goal than to bring to our deaf ears once again the message of the gospel.

CHAPTER THREE

THE MESSAGE OF MEDJUGORJE

The message of Medjugorje is but an echo of the gospel, made actual and applied to the serious situation which has inspired Our Lady's visits.

The Structure of the Message

Medjugorje's message is simple, founded on the gospel, and urgent. For a long time, it baffled the theologian in me because it does not present itself in some easily-formulated manner. It is not destined to be engraved in stone or on walls but *in hearts*. It is at that level that the message must be read. As Paul said in writing to the Corinthians: You are a letter from Christ, written by the Spirit of the living God. (See 2 Corinthians 3:3.)

The message is not conveyed in a systematic way. It is given in a few words:

- A return to God, conversion, faith.
- Prayer, fasting.
- Peace, reconciliation.

This core message was delivered during the very first days before the end of June 1981. Why then, after that, are there so many words and so many apparitions? This is due to the pedagogical formation needed so people could live the message.

People say that the message is banal and repetitive. But education is banal and repetitive. A mother trains her child by repeating elementary and precious things that must be learned about life. It is the same on the spiritual level. Our Lady is playing her role as mother.

The messages received every Thursday by Marija and many messages of Jelena or Ivan are part of this pedagogy. Some of these messages are destined for the prayer group at Medjugorje, others, especially those which Marija receives each Thursday, for the parish. These Thursday messages to Marija are eagerly awaited throughout the world and are disseminated by telephone and written publication.

Those interested may receive information from:

Caritas of Birmingham
Box 120
4647 Highway 280 East
Birmingham, Alabama 35243
Tel: (205) 823-4531

- or -

The Center for Peace
P.O. Box 1269
Concord, Massachusetts 01742
Tel: (617) 371-1235

The message of Medjugorje is supported by signs (healings, divine protection, conversions, phenomena of light and others which awaken or stimulate faith). These signs are intended to help human weakness and inertia. Other aspects of the signs are less important and still not well-understood.

The secrets provide details to the youngsters concerning the grave and urgent reasons for Our Lady's appeal and confer a prophetic sense of the future. The secrets will be made known little by little and, in living them out, the world will understand them. This should take place in a manner similar to that in which the young people are living out the messages: in peace and generosity. We should be on our guard against optical illusions so frequent when there is a question of secrets and eschatology.

In addition to the general messages, there are more particular messages given to one or several of the young people:

-All have received an account (long or short) of Mary's life. Only Vicka seems to have written it down. She plans to publish this when the Virgin gives her permission. This is a disturbing prospect because the "revealed lives" of the Blessed Virgin have always caused problems in the Church, whether it was the account of Mary of Agreda in the 17th century, Catherine Emmerich in the 18th century, or Maria Valtorta in our own century.

-Ivanka, Vicka and others have received teachings that are confidential for the moment. These concern the future of the Church and the world. (I provide some details about these messages in the book *Medjugorje. Récit et message.*)

The manifestation of this obscure, prophetic area (secrets, messages about the future, descriptions of unknown past events) runs the risk of causing more problems some day than most people realize. It is important to point this out at least.

An Analysis of the World's Situation.

This message refers to threats to the world, which will

be more clearly made known as the contents of the ten secrets come to pass. The analysis basically is this: "This world has calmly abandoned itself to sin. It is preparing its own destruction." This is the main point of the secrets.

Upon hearing this, everyone thinks of the threat of an atomic war. It can be understood this way. However, the message has not been that precise, since an atomic war is but one particular outcome of the evil which is eroding humanity. Our century, intoxicated by its scientific and technical success, thinks that its progress is infallible, able to resolve all the world's problems, and even to conquer death. It has gone so far as to think that "the death of God" would free man and accelerate his progress. But, the technological mastery of matter solves only surface problems and not the fundamental problem of humankind, which is the problem of love. Human beings have been created by love, and only love can build up and give order to human beings interiorly. But human love itself can only live by the Love of God the Creator.

This analysis cannot be dismissed with a smile. It confirms and interprets in depth what many great international experts have thought about our planet.

The dangers we face are those of a world in which God does not have His rightful place. Thus, there is constantly more science but less love; more information but less education; more eros but less agape; more intensity but less discipline; more frenetic activity but less peace. We go on at an ever-increasing rate, but toward emptiness and death. The rate of suicides and violent deaths keeps rising. The most obvious danger is clearly the arms race. The military experts of the two superpowers can find no other way of maintaining peace than "the balance of terror." They each

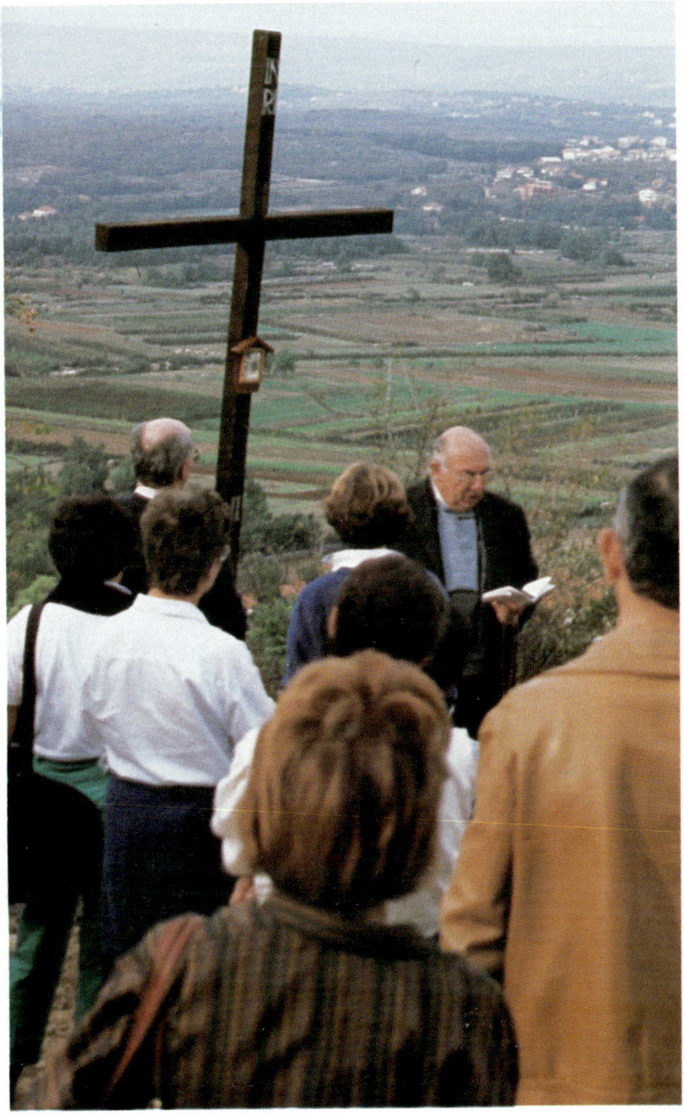
INRI

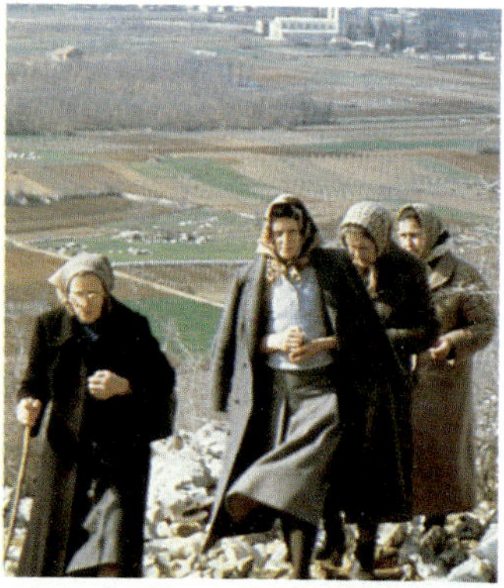

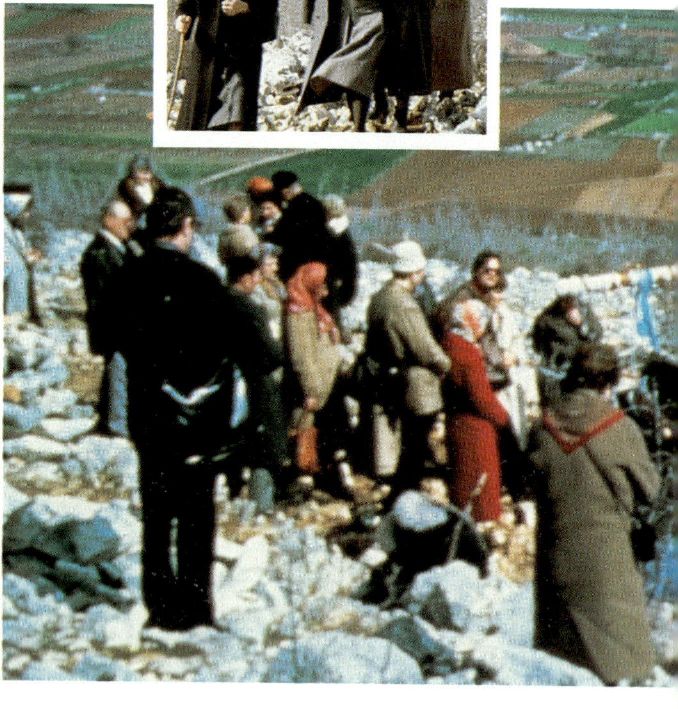

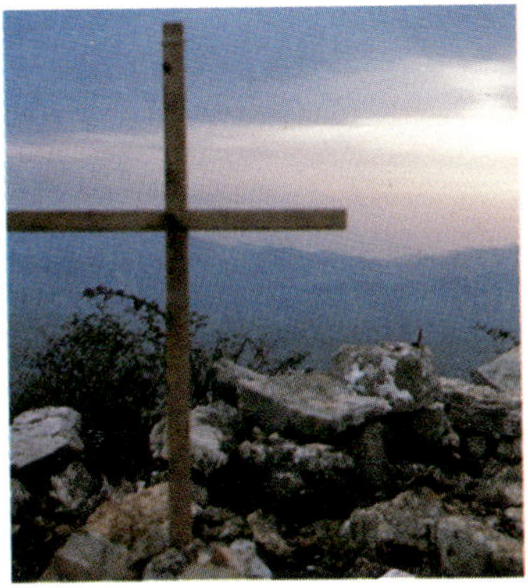

Pilgrims to Medjugorje gather regularly to pray both on the Hill of the Apparitions, where the Virgin first appeared, and on Križevac, the Hill of the Cross.

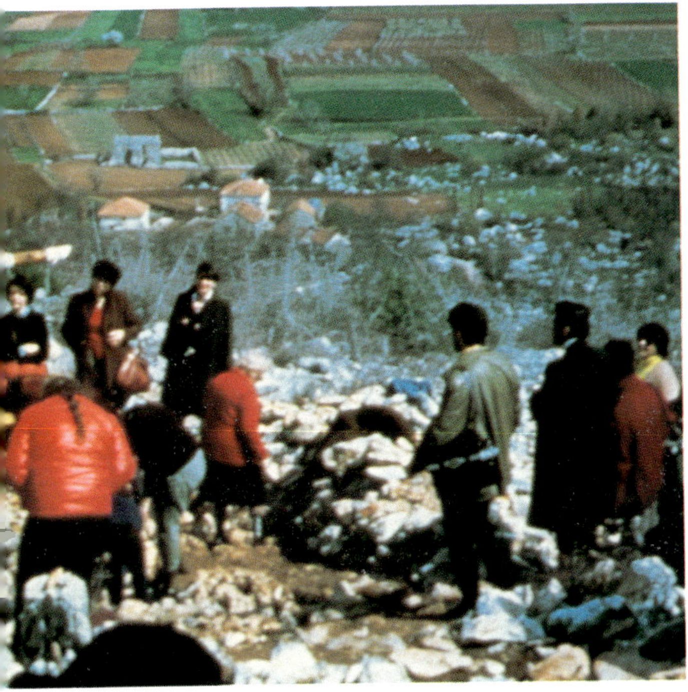

THE VISIONARIES

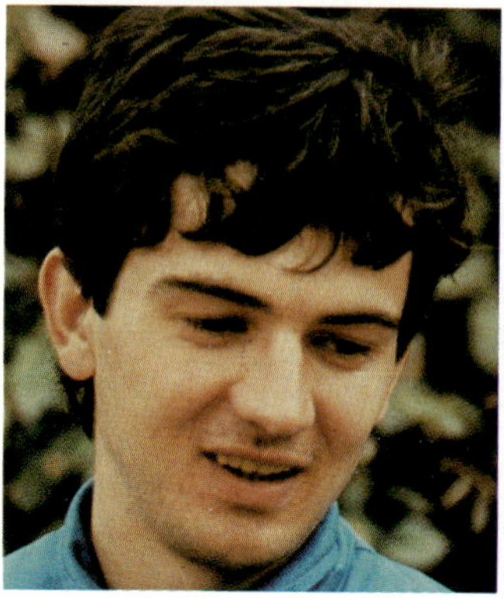

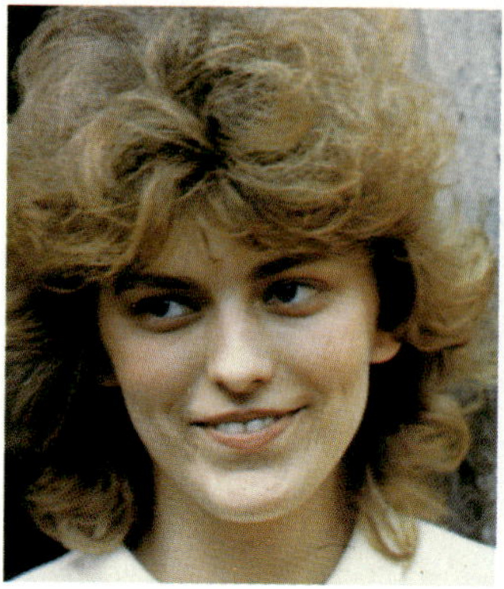

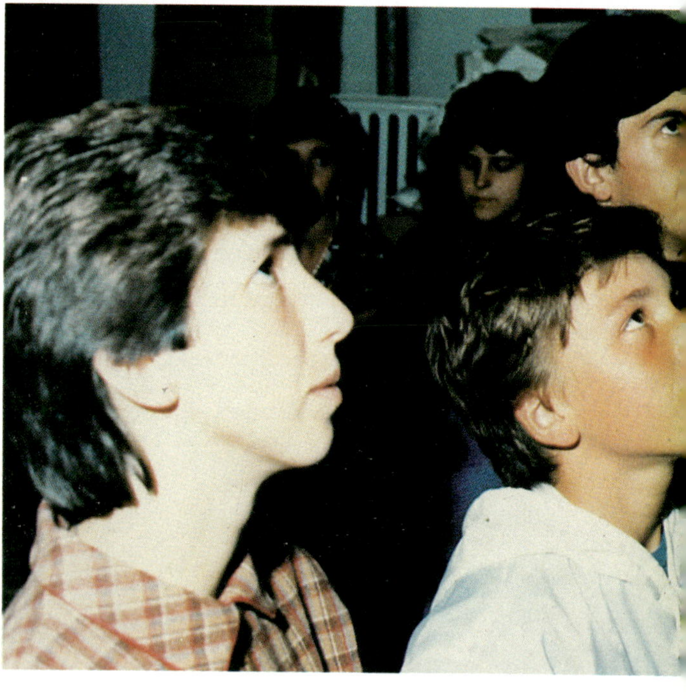

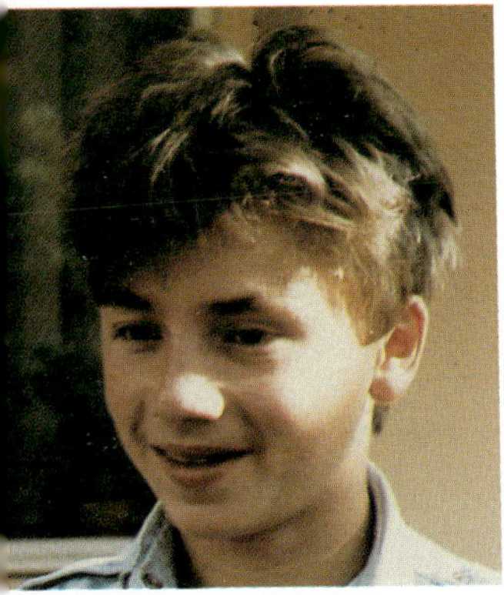

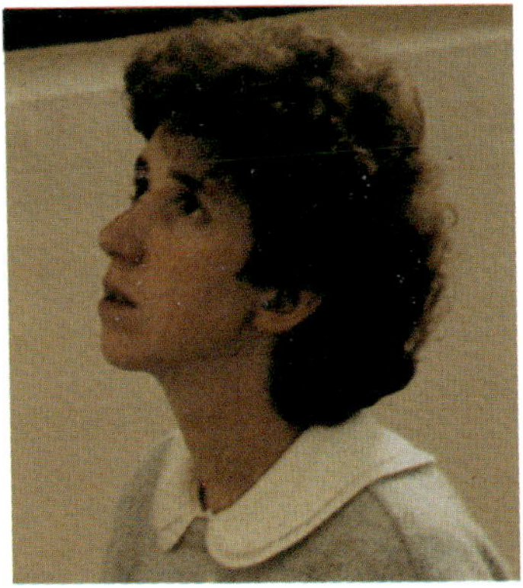

From left to right: Ivan Dragicević, Mirjana Dragicević, Jakov Colo, Marija Pavlović. Below left: Marija, Jakov, and Ivan, during an apparition in late 1985. Below: The six visionaries in December 1982.

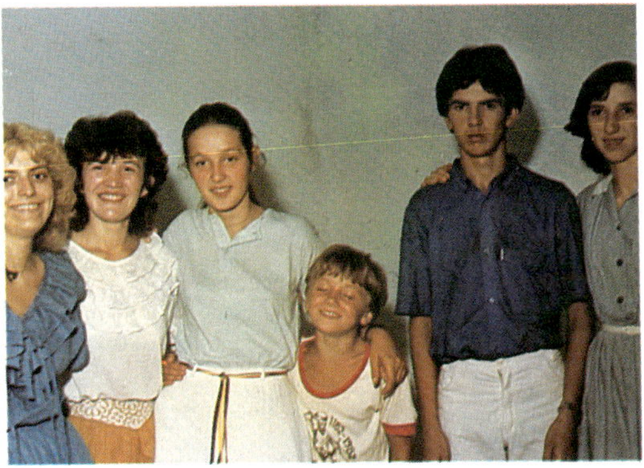

THE VISIONARIES

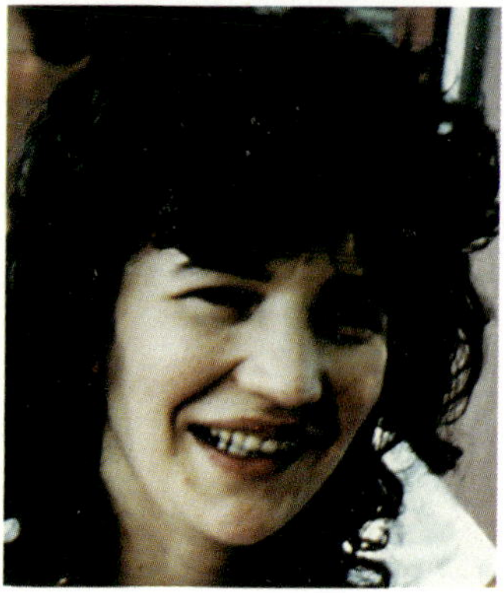

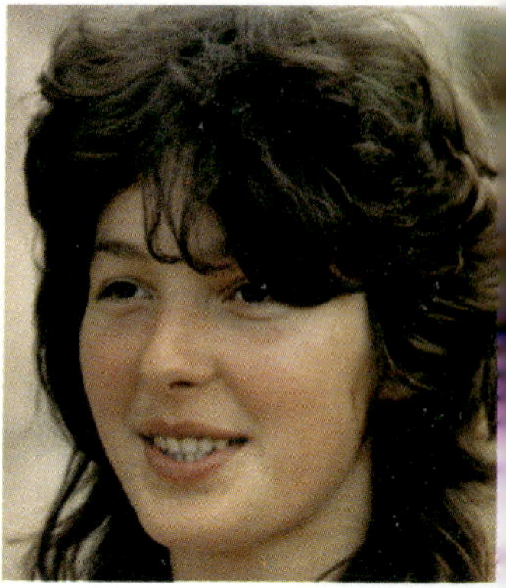

From left to right: Vicka Ivanković, Ivanka Ivanković. Both Jelena Vasilij and Marijana Vasilij hear the Virgin "in their hearts" but do not experience the apparitions. Bottom right: The visionaries during an apparition in December 1982.

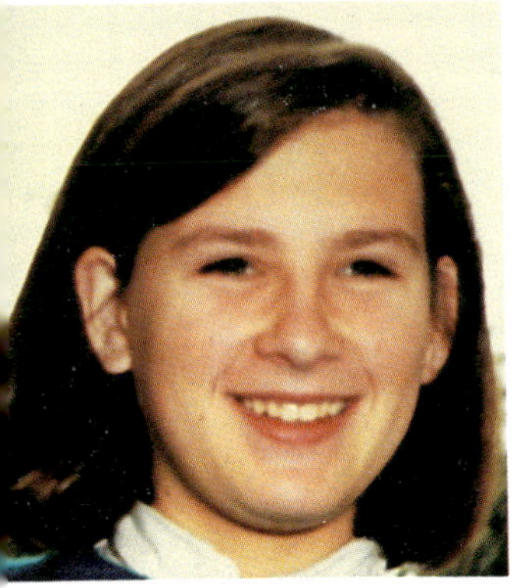
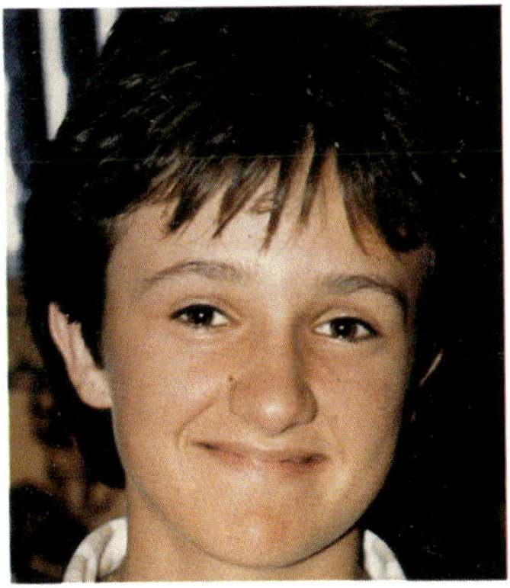
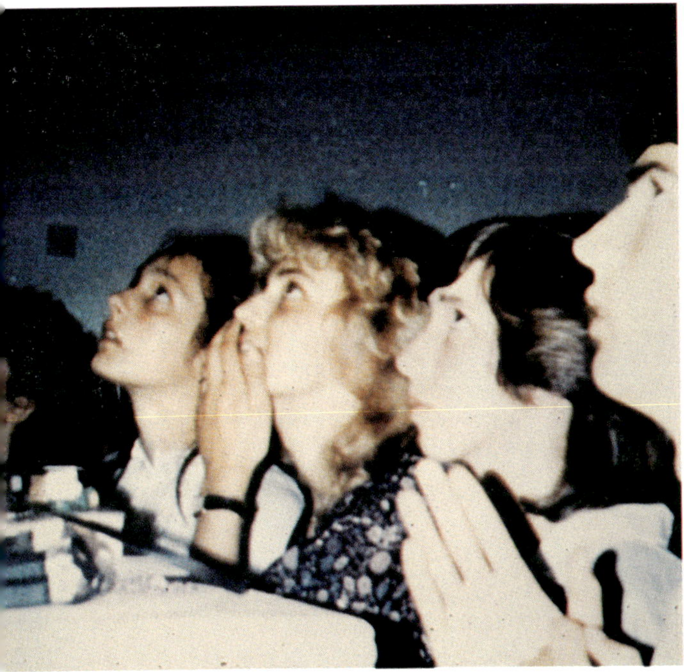

THE PRIESTS

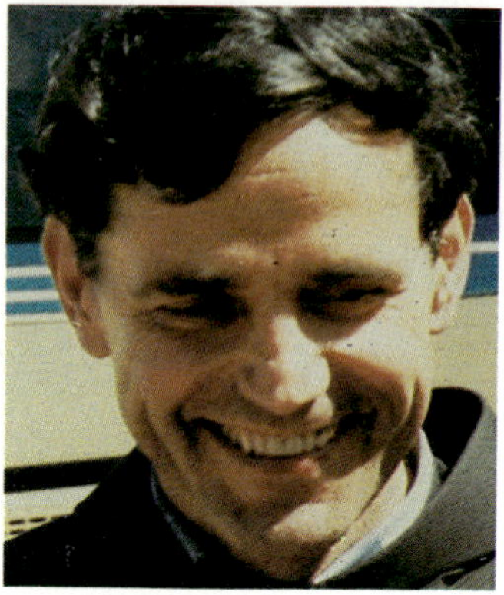

Fr. Jozo Zovko, pastor of St. James until his arrest August 17, 1981.

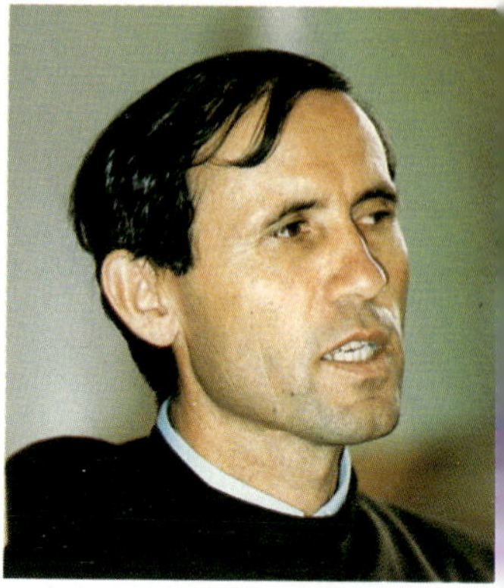

Fr. Tomislav Vlasić, Successor to Fr. Zovko and spiritual guide to the visionaries.

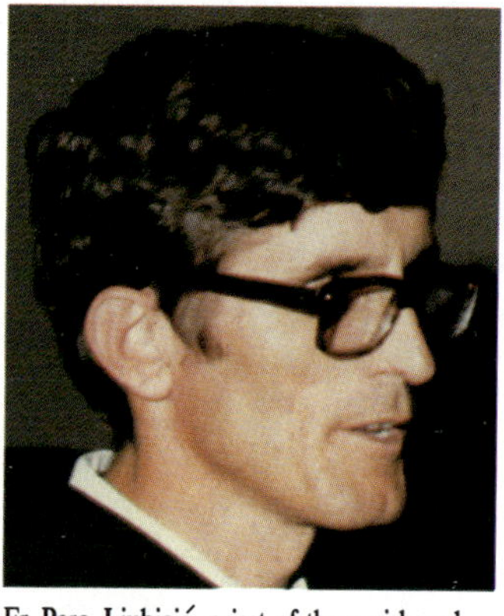

Fr. Pero Ljubicić, priest of the parish and chosen by Mirjana to reveal the secrets.

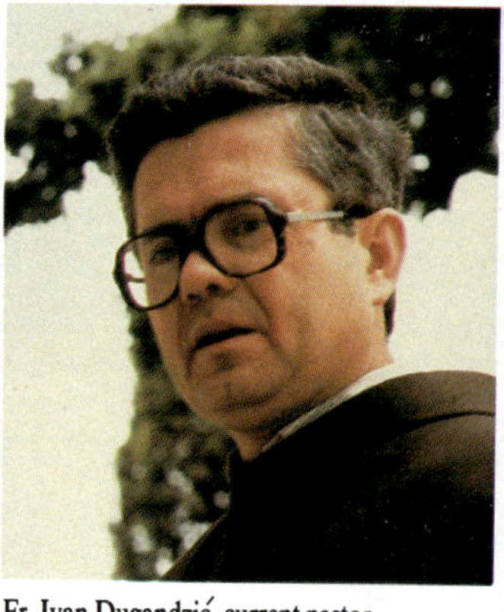

Fr. Ivan Dugandzić, current pastor.

think this way: "If I want to insure peace, I have to be the stronger." Each one then is condemned to surpass the other. There is no reason for this to stop. This mad course has succeeded in multiplying on our planet a greater store of atomic, bacteriological, and chemical armaments than would be required to destroy the whole human race. We have seen over the last twenty years an incredible inability to create a dynamic of peace and disarmament based on values other than the ones prevailing.

However, the Virgin speaks less about these dramatic material expressions than she does about moral disintegration. Love in the genuine sense of the term is growing weak. Desire eclipses the gift of self. Concern to be authentic exempts one from fidelity in commitments. Family life is deeply shaken. It is being replaced by relationships that are both irresponsible and sterile, and which have tripled in the last thirty years among people under thirty.

The number of marriages has noticeably diminished at the same time that the number of divorces has risen sharply. For Protestants, one of three adults have been divorced, and for Catholics, the proportion is one out of every four. In the ten-year period from 1972-1982, there was a 50% increase in the divorce rate among the general population of the United States, and for Catholics in ths country during the same period, the increase in divorces is 90%. 44% of Protestants surveyed in 1985 approved of premarital sex, and 59% of Catholics surveyed approved. Another poll found that only 24% of the Catholic population oppose artifical methods of birth control, compared with 21% of the Protestants surveyed.

The ratio of children to women is getting less and less

while the number of pet dogs and cats has increased so much that it constitutes a problem in some cities. In the Washington, D.C., area, there are three abortions for every two births. The children of divorced couples are real victims. Human beings always avid for love no longer know how to love. Those who love poorly produce those who are poorly loved. Being authentic to the moment is a greater value than fidelity. Good intentions are more important than care for a consistency that provides a real future. None of this is happening without a lot of grief. Sociological studies confirm this. In France, the results of a recent poll of women conducted by the press was greeted with amazement. On the scale of values, the top vote-getter was not what one would have thought: sexual harmony or other similar values. It was fidelity.

In short, our civilization has produced a prodigious development of knowledge, technique, and material proficiency, but stunted its growth in the human realm and more importantly in the divine, which is the deep root of all human authenticity. Despite Nature's ecological rebounding, we pay no attention to balance, particularly in the moral order, and this order is crumbling, much more from within than from the repeated blows of accelerated progress. Progress has too often neglected its service of man and God. It does not build up the genuine human order, which is identical to the divine order and determined by God in whose image he fashioned man.

Thus, with the terrible means at its disposal, the world has become a cultural cauldron, frothing with despair and frustration. From this situation comes the unleashing of violence and all-pervasive insecurity. What we called "progress" at the beginning of the century has provided brand new material for our front pages: drugs, extortion, hijackings, hostage-taking. Our great cities are dangerous places. What was once New York's "prerogative" is now shared by many cities. People avoid going out at night. Many ethnic groups who lived side by side have now transformed their neighborhoods into places of massacre and bloody war, as we can see in Africa and elsewhere.

The world no longer knows where it comes from or where it is going. Having lost the sense of its ultimate destiny, it oscillates between depression and violence.

The Message.

The remedy Our Lady offers is not a miracle falling from the sky, for God has irrevocably placed this world in human hands. That is why He made us free and therefore responsible. The solutions rest in human hands. Created by God, in order to find in God a fullness of love and thus our own fulfillment, humankind must find once again the fundamental solution which alone is able to animate and organize the rest: a return to God, faith, conversion, prayer, fasting, reconciliation, and peace. These key words of the Medjugorje message recall the essential response of the gospel. We have forgotten them. And we must rediscover their fire and light in our own lives. So let us open our hearts.

God.

The heart of Our Lady's message is, first of all, a return to God. "There is only one God," she reminded them as early as June 29, 1981. This truth, badly misunderstood, is the key to all the rest. It is the most often forgotten: God is our Creator. He gives us our very existence. The

Creator is not someone who brought things into existence a long time ago and now does nothing. God continues to create with the same love. If God were not creating us at this very instant, we would cease to exist. We would be like a light bulb when the electricity is turned off. God is closer to us than we are to ourselves.

God has created us free, completely free. We are able to forget Him or even take a stand against Him. But the one who thinks that this is the way to freedom is like the branch which wishes to be free from the tree on which it grows in order to have a better life. When that happens, the branch withers and dies.

God created us to love Him. It is because of love that He gives us existence. He calls us to a love that does not pass away. This is the love Our Lady enkindled so well in the hearts of the young people in Medjugorje. It is the explanation of their joy, harmony, and care about others amid a difficult life.

In our century, spiritual direction has disappeared and psychoanalysis has flourished, founded on the gratification of our primal desires. I would like to see a psychoanalysis based on a deep return to God. This is what makes saints, deep genuineness, and authentic happiness.

Often, we are afraid of God and we run from Him because our lives are not in order with Him. While avoiding the wrong violence to ourselves, let us prepare ourselves to rediscover God:

> Lord, have mercy on me, poor sinner that I am. Help me to change my life, which I don't have the courage to change today.

At the beginning of this century, there was a doctor

who, toward the end of his life, was being led by grace. He would sometimes go into a church and say, "Lord, if You exist, have pity on this poor wretch." And he saw the light.

Conversion.

The call to conversion, issued as early as the apparition of June 26, 1981, refers to a personal act by which we turn to God while turning away from our own ego and from sin. The word "conversion" (in Greek, *metanoia*) is well-illustrated in ski jargon where a conversion is a hundred-and-eighty-degree change of direction while coming down a slope. It is an about-face from a wrong direction to a right one. This becomes easy once we realize that God is really everything.

"I am he who am, you are she who is not," the Lord once said to St. Catherine of Sienna.

God is the beginning and end of our existence, our origin and our future. Independently of any decision of ours, every fiber of our being is a gift from God. If we are unaware of this very nature of our being, we live life as it comes along, often anxiously pursuing one vanity after another without rhyme or reason. To be converted means to recognize that God is first in our lives. It is to acknowledge gratefully that He is the abiding and loving source of our existence. Conversion is not a return to some past, a nostalgic search for the maternal womb. It is rather a dynamic movement toward Love who calls us to love.

Conversion is turning from the self-centeredness of sin in order to turn to God because He is the deepest and most mysterious Truth of our being, the power and the light by which we attain to God day by day.

Conversion therefore means consecration with its twofold aspect of God's primary work in us and our work in God, for God can do nothing in us without our consent.

Consecration is first of all a gift from God. Only God can consecrate us, that is, make us his, make us saints, cause us to live in him and unite us to himself in his holiness. God does this in the unique and radical act of baptism. From that moment, our being is fundamentally consecrated. However, unfortunately, our life is not consecrated. Our desires push and pull us in every direction often outside of God or opposed to Him.

It remains for us to change, to consecrate ourselves completely, at each moment of our lives and with each fiber of our being, so that our life finds its meaning, its harmony and its fulfillment in God our Creator. In order to bring this about, God is continually at work in us, causing the initial grace of baptism to bear fruit. He heals us and stirs up our freedom. He purifies, transforms and completes our whole being so that He can love us without reserve.

By calling us to conversion, Mary is thus urging us to yield to that action of the Holy Spirit within us by which we honestly assess our lives in the light of the cross of our Lord Jesus Christ. If we will let Him teach us, we will see our true state and beg God to come to our help so that we can turn from sin and embrace His new life. Mary sees God clearly and this vision allows her to grasp the deep inroads made in our personalities by our habit patterns of sin and our easy acceptance of compromise. She knows that unless we beg the Lord to come to our help and change us, no other grace or healing or wonder will ultimately profit us. As a good disciple, Mary is but repeating the words of her Son recorded in the gospel of St. Mark: "The time is fulfilled and the kingdom of God is at hand. Repent and believe the good news" (Mark 1:15). Repent, not only to avoid chastisement, but in order to receive through faith the life that comes from Jesus Christ.

Faith.

The return to God is brought about by faith. The messages of the first days stressed this: "I have come because there are strong believers here" [June 26, 1981]. "Happy are those who have not seen and who believe" [June 26]. "That the people believe and persevere in faith" [June 27]. There are many other similar exhortations.

By faith, we adhere to God, His word, and His truth. When we believe, our lives make sense again and are consistent. Faith still leaves us in the dark, but it is a night strewn with stars. God does not leave those who put their whole trust in Him without some sign of His presence and care.

Faith involves not only an intimate relationship with God, Our Father, but also with mankind. God is the father of all men and He invites us to go out to meet and serve our brothers and sisters—those who are near or far, and those who are hungry. In this latter activity, fasting, of which we will speak later, can be a help.

We should be on guard against an illusion rather current in our time which can be expressed in the formula: "Works of charity first: God will come along afterward." This may happen once in a while by way of exception, but the normal road, the royal road, leads to God first as the source of all the rest. He alone can instill and create love in us, whereas works of charity without God soon wilt and weaken. Whenever Mother Teresa and her sisters have expended their last ounce of strength and courage in their ceaseless work with lepers and the dying, they have an hour of adoration before the Blessed Sacrament. Thus, that fullness of love which is in God is renewed in them. Thank you, Mother Teresa, for having reminded us of this truth when we had forgotten it.

Prayer.

Prayer is the normal language of faith, the expression of a life in common with God.

Prayer has been the very fabric of the apparitions from the beginning, when the young people understood that they had to pray in order to welcome Our Lady or to ask her to return after she had disappeared. At each apparition, they pray with her, saying the "Our Father" and the "Glory Be," which she begins and they take up. The children's voices, which disappear during the ecstasy, reappear when they pray. This points to the value which Our Lady places on prayer. It is the high point of the apparitions, when we all pray with her. At Medjugorje, the life of prayer began with a tradition of vocal prayer: seven of the "Our Father," "Hail Mary" and "Glory Be" along with some familiar hymns that Our Lady sings with the youngsters. It was not long before the prayers at the apparitions led into the prayer of the Mass which followed them and now completes them every day.

Mary issues an invitation to return to true prayer, the "prayer of the heart." Jelena and Ivan received this directive from her to transmit to their prayer group and by extension to everyone else.

Prayer is more than asking for things. It is communication with God which begins with a certain quietness and peace by which we prepare ourselves to receive God in the depths where He abides in us. This dialogue is not monotonous but takes on many tones. In the old days, when people were taught a method for prayer, the basic attitudes of prayer were summed up in the acronym ATPOR:

Adoration
Thanksgiving
Petition
Offering
Resolution

Using these attitudes as a starting point, let us discuss prayer:

Adoration of the Creator. This is of prime and capital importance. We may kneel, prostrate, stretch our arms out in the form of a cross. These and other gestures can help since our body, too, must enter into this movement of communication with God.

Thanksgiving. This indicates a quality that is not common among us, namely, gratitude. Our gratitude must go out and up to God first of all because of who He is and, secondly, because of what He has done for us. Although we "give" this thanks to God, we are not left without it. Rather, it increases in this new contact with God Himself.

Petition. This is what we usually think of first when we think of prayer. But, really, it is less a question of asking and more that of receiving the gift of God. You must learn to say to Him: "Lord, what do you want me to do? What are you saying to me today?" God does have something to tell us. The problem is that we do not listen. Prayer finds its proper harmony and effectiveness when we understand God's desires, no matter how great they may be, regarding the world and us. When we thus understand God's desires, we have a hope that does not disappoint us.

Besides asking those things from God which we need and seeking from Him an understanding of His plan for our lives and what He wants to give us, we have another very precious way of asking questions of God. The Lord wants us to go and ask Him to explain the meaning of the death and resurrection of His Son. Our Lord Jesus, Himself, desires that we look to Him with confidence and ask Him to teach us the depths of what the scriptures say about Him. He wants us to ask Him: "Lord, why did you have to die?" "Lord, how does your death on the cross bring about a change in my life?" "Lord, teach me about your majesty and authority. Teach me what heaven will be like." This form of petition is one that delights the heart of God.

Offering. Prayer is a gift of the self. Our lives and our deaths are irreplaceable sacrifices which no one else can perform for us. Such a consecration constitutes the priesthood of all the faithful, be they priests or lay people. Our offering reaches its fulfillment for each one of us in the total sacrifice of death, that final and most precious act of our whole lives because it identifies us deeply with the cross of Christ and brings us into the fulfillment of His love.

Resolution. Prayer is not window-shopping, poetry, or flights of our imagination concerning God and heaven. It is rather a commitment of our will to be rooted in God, a way of life enlightened by the Holy Spirit and adjusted to the realities of this world.

This basic outline of prayer presumes a foundational reality. To pray is not only to recognize that one is a creature come forth from the hands of a transcendent God, it is also to recognize that one is a sinner before the holy

God. This should not produce in us panic or despair, but rather hope and boundless gratitude because the recognition of ourselves as sinners takes place in light of the mercy of God, and in light of His love which takes the initiative and is inexhaustible. The Lord Himself said so in this astonishing phrase from the Gospel: "I tell you there will be more joy in heaven over one repentant sinner than over ninety-nine righteous people who have no need to repent." (Luke 15:7.)

The closer we come to the Lord, the more we see our faults. Jelena recently confided: "When the Gospa told us to go to confession every month, I thought that was a lot. I really had to think hard to come up with some sins I had committed. But it is curious, the more she helps me grow, and the closer I come to God, the more sins I discover because I see more clearly."

Yes, we make our way to God dressed in our misery. But it is in this state that He loves us and it is in this way that the light of His love can transform us. The Pharisee's self-sufficiency prevents God's mercy from penetrating. The publican's humility is an open gate to the flood of God's love. If God causes us to desire Him in the very depths of our being, it is so that He can satisfy that desire which He has awakened in us. Mary expressed this beautifully when she said: "My being proclaims the greatness of the Lord, my spirit finds joy in God my Savior, for He has looked upon His servant in her lowliness; all ages to come shall call me blessed. God who is mighty has done great things for me, holy is His name." (Luke 1:46-49.)

Fasting.

What shall we say about fasting? We shall have to spend

more time on this topic, not because it is more important, but because it is the key to the rest—a key we had lost. After all these centuries during which fasting became a formality and finally eroded away, it is not easy to understand it once again. But it is with joy and fruitfulness that fasting has been rediscovered not only by the youngsters but by more than 1,000 parishioners at Medjugorje and over 100,000 pilgrims who have visited there.

Our Lady spoke about this topic, as she did about the preceding topics, during the second apparition on the hillside. It was Marija who received this message in this order: "You must believe, pray, FAST, and go to confession." Fasting was inserted between prayer and confession.

Our Lady's word found an immediate echo. On Thursday, July 2, a few days after the first apparitions, the pastor Fr. Jozo Zovko, confused by all the events proposed to his parishioners, assembled for Mass: "Do you agree that we should fast for three days in order to ask for light?"

For months, he had been trying to restore the ancient Franciscan custom of fasting on bread and water. No one listened to him, not even members of the Third Order. But on that day, the crowd that filled the church for the weekday Mass was large and enthusiastic. They responded: "Yes, we agree!"

On July 21, 1982, in answer to a question from Fr. Tomislav Vlašić, Our Lady supplied the following particulars:

The best fast is on bread and water.

Fasting can avert war.

Fasting can suspend natural laws.

These last two points may seem surprising, but they

echo the gospel teaching about the faith that "can move mountains" (Matthew 17:20) and about demons that can only be cast out by prayer and fasting (Mark 9:29, an ancient reading of the text).

Fasting! The prospect may seem frightening but it is really good news.

When we are invited to a big meal at some celebration, we call that good news even though the overeating is going to weigh us down. During the Christmas holidays, I hear people say: "I hope all these parties are over soon." Their stomachs and their livers need a rest.

To be invited to fast is good news of another kind and it is a gift. We are called to fast from sin and the occasions of sin. By fasting from food as well, we add intensity to our prayer and are more deeply identified with the fasting and suffering of Jesus and the hunger and pain of so many of our brothers and sisters in today's world. Fasting is also good for our health. It eliminates toxins and burns away excess fat. Those who fast regularly appreciate its benefits. Their minds are clearer and they may prolong their lives.

Our Lady has told the youngsters to fast on bread and water twice a week. This may not be for all nor is it possible for everyone to undertake something like this from the outset. I refer the reader to Appendix II for a longer discussion of the subject. For more details on the subject of fasting, I refer as well to *Scientific and Medical Studies on the Apparitions at Medjugorje*, Dublin: Veritas, 1987, pp. 77-97.

Peace and Reconciliation.

This is a well-conceived plan: the return to God through

faith, conversion, prayer, and fasting leads to reconciliation and peace, the key words of Medjugorje.

"Peace, Peace, Peace!" "Be reconciled!" (June 26, 1981.) From the very beginning, this has been the final word of the message.

"Peace, Peace, Peace!" "Nothing but peace!" Our Lady repeated this to Marija the same day and she showed her the Cross of Christ. She went on to say: "Make peace with God and among yourselves."

Each apparition concludes with this farewell so full of meaning:

"Go in the peace of God."

The root of all division is our broken relationship with God. This is why we are so often divided within ourselves and with others.

To return to God, our Creator and our Savior, is to find once again our own interior unity and our ability to be reconciled with others. It can be a long, slow process. Often, we have habit patterns of deep resentment. We need to ask God in prayer to give us a *healing of memories*. This is a great spiritual benefit. It is a veritable liberation. It allows us to pray wholeheartedly for those who wish evil towards us, and to love our enemies as the gospel enjoins us.

We must also learn to see the good in those who commit evil and to forgive the evil in them. This is the practice of justice according to our Lord's parable about the speck in our neighbor's eye and the beam in our own. It is the secret of spiritual effectiveness, for only good can remedy evil. If we begin with our gifts and good qualities, we can overcome our faults which are found primarily in our incapacities and deficiencies.

We cannot put the cart before the horse. In order to be reconciled with others, we must first of all be reconciled with ourselves. And in order to be reconciled to ourselves, we must be reconciled with God, who restores our strength and our unity and who is the author of our freedom itself.

All of this is but the call of the gospel. Our Lady has come to repeat it to our deaf ears. It is the abiding secret of well-being and happiness. It is the secret of every healing, and this is all the more urgent at a time when the disease of sin is claiming spiritual and bodily deaths in ever greater numbers.

The way of truth produces its profound effect. The return of so many Christians to prayer, conversion, and fasting has delayed the evils that were threatening the world and has mitigated the cataclysm revealed but not yet disclosed in the seventh secret, according to the testimony of the young people. That is why the serious message of Medjugorje has nothing dramatic about it. The young people hesitate between two statements which are perhaps complementary:

The punishments are (in part) inevitable.

Fasting and prayer can avert war and calamity.

The important point lies beyond this seeming ambiguity because for those who enter into the way of God's love, all things work together for good (Romans 8:28), and everything will end well. The young people at Medjugorje have understood that there is no longer anything to fear.

The Virgin Mary recalls to our world in danger the urgency of her message. It is from her that we have the good news of the birth of Jesus, the Son of God, who became her son (Luke 1:28-35) and, because of this, became one of us, our brother. Through this mother—the mother of

God and our mother—divine love has entered our world. Because of that birth, humanity has become virtually the body of Christ and an extension of the Trinity, that eternal sharing of love.

By her faith, the Virgin Mary tenderly formed the physical body of Christ and, at the same time, provided the foundation for his mystical body of which she is the first member.

Today, she comes to remind us of this good news at a very serious moment before that moment becomes and, indeed, so that it may not become, an hour of distress. Her call has been listened to in Yugoslavia, Italy, Austria, and elsewhere. In France, the call has not been so well-heard because of the conspiracy of silence and the many calumnies which have become solidly established. Nevertheless, in France as elsewhere, the tree is producing only good fruit which itself wards off the threats of death of which Mary warns us. What happens now depends upon us. We hold the cards: it is up to us to choose between the unbridled vanities which seduce us and God; between self-centeredness and love; between our petty preoccupations and the future of humankind; between our childish illusions and the eternal future of God.

Thus will the truth, dead in so many hearts, become a living truth that saves.

APPENDIX I

THE MESSAGE AND TEACHING METHODS OF OUR LADY AT MEDJUGORJE

The Message

At the very first apparitions in june 1981, Mary delivered the message of Medjugorje. It can be found running through the narrative given above in Chapter One and is synthesized in the conclusion on pages 55-57: the return to God, conversion, repentance, faith, prayer, fasting, penance, peace, and reconciliation. The secrets adapt this message to the urgency of the world situation.

Teaching Methods and Pastoral Care

The reason for the astonishing abundance of communications from Our Lady is so that they will become part of the lives of the young people who see the apparitions and part of the lives of the parish and of the pilgrims who hear the message and reap its fruits.

The prolongation of the apparitions and the multitude of words is explained by this pedagogical work which is so admirable. The simple gospel words of the message take on their full meaning when they are put into practice. They are the words of a mother. They have no meaning except in a genuine relationship with this loving and clear-speaking mother. Many have taken up these words and experienced their fruit. That is why means of diffusing these messages were spontaneously organized in several countries. In the United States, there are among other organizations:

The Riehle Foundation
P.O. Box 7
Milford, Ohio 45150
Tel: (513) 831-8068

- or -

Caritas of Birmingham
Box 120, 4647 Highway 280 East,
Birmingham, Alabama 35243
Tel: (205) 823-4531

- or -

The Center for Peace
P.O. Box 1269,
Concord, Massachusetts 01742
Tel: (617) 371-1235

A book is currently in preparation on the whole of Medjugorje's message which is the essence of all the rest. While awaiting its publication, we find it sufficient here to give a few samplings of the teaching messages confided to Jelena at irregular intervals and to Marija on a regular basis:

Jelena does not belong to the group of the six young

people who see the apparitions; however, since mid-December 1982, she has been receiving communications, sometimes perceiving Our Lady "in her heart." Her messages have had a considerable influence on the parish, especially in regard to the celebration of the two-thousandth anniversary of the birth of Mary, August 5, 1984, which was marked by an extraordinary outpouring of grace, conversions, and confessions.

Marija's messages, which began on March 1, 1984, were being received each Thursday with one or two exceptions until January 8, 1987, when the messages became monthly on the 25th of each month.

Jelena's Messages

These began in 1983 and have had a great influence on the parish. Some examples are given here:

April 20, 1983: I want to convert them but they are not converting. Pray, pray for them. Do not wait. I need your prayers and your penance.

June 16: I have come to tell the world that God is truth, that He exists. In Him is to be found true happiness and the fullness of life [...] Peace is needed for the salvation of the world. In God, true joy is found. From this flows true peace.

June 22: Love your enemies and pray for them.

June 28: Pray three hours each day. You pray too little. At least pray a half-hour morning and night.

July 4: You have begun to pray three hours, but you look at your watch, concerned about your work. Be concerned with the essential. Let yourself be guided in a deep way by the Holy Spirit. Then your work will go well.

July 26: Be alert. This is a dangerous time for you. The devil will try to divert you from this path. Those who give themselves to God will be subject to attack.

August 2: Consecrate yourselves to the Immaculate Heart. Just abandon yourselves. I will protect you. I will pray to the Holy Spirit. You pray to Him as well.

January 27, 1984: Pray and fast. I desire that you draw your life from the well of prayer. You must pray every morning, upon awakening, the prayer of consecration to the Heart of Mary.

February 23: It is for you to pray. It is for me to look after all the rest. You cannot understand the purity of God. For that, pray, pray, pray. For He desires to be with you and to purify you from all sin.

March 1: Every Thursday, let each one fast in one way or another. Let those who smoke abstain from smoking. Let those who drink alcohol abstain from alcohol. As for the others, let them give up something which is dear to them. If anyone desires to sanctify a day in a special way, let him fast that day. These recommendations should be passed on to the parishioners.

After the end of February, Jelena's messages do not concern the parish so much as her prayer group, which Our Lady is leading in both a demanding and discreet way. Jelena's messages, therefore, are no longer spread abroad.

Marija's Messages

On March 1, 1984, Marija began to receive messages

every Thursday, and these have been widely disseminated. Again, some examples will be given here:

March 1, 1984: My dear children, I have specially chosen this parish and I want to guide it. I watch over it in love and I want all of you to be mine. I thank you for your response this evening. I desire that there always be many of you with me and my Son. I will give you a message each Thursday.

March 8: I thank you for having answered my call. Dear children, be converted in this parish. This is my second desire. Thus, all who come here will be able to be converted.

November 29: My dear chidren, you do not yet know how to love.

January 31, 1985: My dear children, today, I want to ask you to open your hearts to God: flowers at springtime open themselves to the sun. I am your mother and I wish to see you always closer to your Father and I desire that He fill your hearts with many gifts.

November 7: I call upon you to love your neighbor, especially those who do evil to you. In this way, you will be able to discern with love the intentions of hearts. Pray and love, dear children. It is through the power of love that you will be able to accomplish the impossible.

January 9, 1986: I call upon you to help Jesus with your prayer for the realization of all the plans He has already begun to realize here. Offer your sacrifices to Jesus so that He can bring to pass all that He has planned so that Satan would be able to do nothing.

February 27: Live in humility.

October 16: I would like [...] to show you how much I love you, but I am saddened at not being able to make you understand my love. That is why I call you to prayer and to a complete abandonment to God. Satan wants to trap you in your daily affairs and take the first place in your lives. Thus, dear children, pray without ceasing.

January 8, 1987: Dear children, I thank you for your responses to my messages [...] especially for the sacrifices and prayers you have offered.

Dear children, from now on, I will give you messages not every Thursday but on each 25th of the month. The time has come when all that my Lord willed has been accomplished. After today, I will give you fewer messages, but I am with you. That is why, dear children, I beg of you, listen to my messages and live them out. It is in this way that I can guide you. Thank you, my dear children, for having responded to my call.

January 25, 1987: (First monthly message.)

Dear children, today I call upon you to begin a new life from this moment. Understand that God has chosen each one of you to carry out His great plan for the salvation of humanity. You cannot understand how great your role is in the plan of God. That is why you must pray, my dear children, and you will come to know in prayer the plan of God through you. I am with you so that this plan can be fully achieved. Thank you for having answered my call.

APPENDIX II

FASTING

I wish to discuss here, in a briefer form and for English-speaking readers, many of the things I said in the book, *Scientific and Medical Studies on the Apparitions at Medjugorje* (Dublin: Veritas, 1987, pp. 77-97).

One principle with which we may begin is that our systems may take some time to adjust to fasting and it might be wise to approach it in stages. It is probably better to limit the fast to once a week at least at the outset. This could even be demanded by the frantic pace of our lives today. Fasting does not agree with the drive, tension, and overloaded schedules that characterize modern life. According to samplings taken at various conferences, those who fast once a week (more than 100,000 if I recall) are decidedly more numerous than those who fast twice a week. Marija (one of the young people), who had increased her fasts to three times a week plus long fasts before major feast days, ran into health problems. Her doctor and her spiritual director told her to limit her fasting. Fasting requires peace and relaxation (not the same as inactivity). It is often difficult to find days that are appropriate for it. Also, the system must adapt itself gradually to fasting and everyone needs to find the type of fast that provides maximum effectiveness for prayer, work, personal relationships, and so forth. Fasting is not masochism. Normally, the fast day should not be characterized by moods or ineffective activity. If the work undertaken must be done more calmly, and at a quieter pace, and is perhaps a bit constricted by side effects, it also usually turns out to be more effective work.

There can be medical reasons for not fasting. Professor Joyeux "strongly dissuades pregnant women, nursing mothers, and those engaged in heavy labor or who drive heavy trucks" from fasting. In this last category, once again, it all depends on how well one can adapt. Mr. and Mrs. Karminsky once chauffeured me on their day of fast (a fairly radical 24-hour fast) and they maintained their composure throughout. However, it is true that they have years of experience and know their limits.

There may be psychological reasons for not fasting. Someone suffering from anxiety could easily become obsessed with being hungry and be unable to do anything. He will not experience the benefits of fasting and he will become irritable. Such a person should not force himself psychologically. He should prepare himself for fasting, beginning with very moderate attempts, and do everything to make it easy. Usually someone who fasts is not hungry. At most, he will know *moments* when the stomach feels pinched, but these illusory hunger pangs disappear in a few seconds provided the person does not concentrate on this tiny side effect. It is rather a psychological phenomenon which increases the more we think of it, but disappears as soon as our thoughts are focused on something else.

For people who have delicate health or some other special reason, the fast can be adapted. For instance, some people find that fasting entails a depressing headache, a result of hypoglycemia (lack of sugar). In such cases, one should avoid taking pieces of sugar or sweet drinks. For other reasons, alcohol and any artificial foods should be avoided; they are contrary to the spirit of fasting. Coffee is not recommended, although some very solid people have recourse to a stimulant to enable fasting to take place within a life that is irremediably tense and fast-paced. But these are fringe cases better excused than imitated.

Fruits in season are recommended. They are natural and economical nourishment in keeping with poverty as are bread and water. They are a better way to cure headaches due to hypoglycemia and also can be helpful to those who suffer from constipation as a result of fasting. Along the same lines, the sisters at the rectory in Medjugorje cook vegetables for those who need them (no meat, of course). Adaptations such as these can be stages in developing a capacity to fast.

Some people compensate for these compromises by undertaking, perhaps once a month, a more radical fast of water alone. This fast has excellent purifying effects for the body and soul and some people can do this with no more difficulty than fasting on bread and water. It is worth trying to do this from time to time, be it only on Good Friday. This is an adaptation of the fast that goes in the radical direction.

Those who find the psychological, social, or other burdens too great to allow for a fast of bread and water can at least fast from meat and follow the advice given by Jelena "for every Thursday":

Let those who smoke abstain from smoking.

Let those who drink alcohol abstain from alcohol.

For the others, let them give up something that is dear to them (March 1, 1984).

She also said: "Fast from television as well; that is a

bondage that makes prayer impossible."

Fasting also means abstaining from moods and overly aggressive behavior. It involves making ourselves available to serve others. By fasting, we husband our resources to help the poor and the hungry. This was one of the important motivations behind the great popular fasts undertaken in the Philippines in the past two years.

However, the primary function of fasting is something else. The emptiness in our stomach opens us to God; it makes us better disposed to prayer and gives us more time for it. In families where everyone fasts, it means a day off for the woman of the house, who does not have to cook meals and wash dishes. It is the spirit of the fast which matters, but we should not say that *only* the spirit matters. Our prayer and our spiritual experience reside in a body. They follow the body's rhythms and are dependent upon it. Depriving the body can awaken the hunger of the soul. Lanza del Vasto once expressed this very well. On the days when he fasted only on bread and water, he used to say: "Lord, today you will be my only bread."

Fasting can be a good springboard for prayer, charity, peace, and reconciliation. Well understood, a fast is pacifying.

For centuries, those who practiced authentic fasting experienced its benefits. These are some of the things Pope St. Leo said in his sermons concerning fasting:

> Fasting promotes health amid freedom and freedom amid health for while the flesh is governed by the ascendancy of the spirit, the spirit is governed by the help of God (Sermon 1,2).

> Fasting gives birth to pure thoughts, reasonable deci-

sions and salutary counsels (Sermon 13,1).

St. Leo places less emphasis on the salutary function of fasting and more on the fact that it opens us to God and to others:

> Let everyone recognize in himself his mortal, mutable and perishable condition and because of this common condition, let him show to his neighbor a brother's love (Sermon 11,1).

> Let the abstinence of the one who fasts become food for the poor man (Sermon 13,1).

From the practical and medical points of view, fasting on bread and water poses no problem. There is normally no need to be under medical supervision as would be the case for more radical and prolonged fasts. But some precautions are necessary. Dr. Joyeux listed these in *Scientific and Medical Studies*, pp. 95-96. The main considerations are the following:

Be sure to drink at least a quart and a half of water during the day. This is needed for balance and proper elimination.

Whole wheat bread is preferable.

I would add: do not stuff yourself with bread; you will be depriving yourself of the major benefits of the fast: purification of the body and the mind, elimination of toxins and excess fats and, finally, that sense of freedom which unburdens both body and soul.

Each one will have to decide how to resolve the minor, secondary problems stemming from fasting. We have already suggested fruit for those who suffer from headaches due to hypoglycemia. Usually, however, after a certain period of time, the body adapts to fasting and no longer needs fruit. Fasting may entail passing *moments* of light depression which create the sense of needing a nap. It can happen at times that we are actually living on nervous energy and are in need of sleep. In that case, fasting provides us with an invitation to take some additional rest and regain a healthier state.

For most people, the day following a fast is one of extra energy. The body is purified, rested, and rebuilt by the general lull it experienced. It is now relaxed and ready to resume a normal rhythm. In the book *Scientific and Medical Studies*, which we wrote together, Dr. Joyeux told me to cross out "extra" energy. But at that time, he was only a beginner at fasting. I do not think that today he would contest the point.

It is up to you, therefore, to see how you will enter into this experience which hundreds of thousands of Christians are discovering. It is not merely a question of health. Fasting is more importantly a spiritual function resting on a bodily foundation. This privation generates and awakens a certain desire which can be turned into a hunger and thirst for God himself. It provides extra time which can be given to prayer and the service of others.

APPENDIX III

VISITS TO MEDJUGORJE

(The following is adapted from an article which appeared in Chrétiens, *January/March, 1987.)*

On January 31, 1987, the Italian press, and then the French press carried the announcement: "From now on, pilgrimages to Medjugorje are prohibited."

This marks the third time that this has happened, and each time it has been necessary to publish a denial. The false report stems each time from the same source, the Bishop of Mostar. The Bishop is anxious to have the Medjugorje pilgrimages suppressed (to this date about 10 million pilgrims have visited there) and, therefore, he circulates, with the help of some well-placed friends in Rome, reports which dissuade pilgrims from going to Medjugorje.

The false report took undue advantage of a communiqué, issued on January 9, 1987, which bore the signatures of Cardinal Kuharić, President of the Yugoslav Bishops Conference, and Bishop Žanić of Mostar.

Why these two signatures? The Cardinal's was there because judgment on the Medjugorje apparitions has been transferred to the national episcopal conference of which he is the president. As for the Bishop of Mostar, from whom Rome removed responsibility for judging the case because of his negative bias, his signature was present because he is a member of the episcopal conference and the

Bishop of the diocese where the apparitions are occurring.

The object of the communiqué was to announce the transfer of competence and the erection of a new commission of inquiry. Bishop Žanić requested that the prohibition against official pilgrimages be recalled on this occasion, and he proposed a number of somewhat radical formulations which were modified by the episcopal conference.

The resulting compromise is obscure. After having recalled, "the prudence required in such circumstances," the communiqué goes on to state:

"The organization of pilgrimages motivated by the supernatural character attributed to the phenomena at Medjugorje is not authorized."

The text is ambiguous. Some people understood it to mean: If you go to Medjugorje for purposes of tourism on the Dalmatian coast, or mountain climbing on Križevac hill, or enjoying the food of the restaurants of that area, you are on the side of the law. If, however, you go for "supernatural" motives, to pray, fast, or be converted, you are going against the decree of the Church.

Obviously, this interpretation is absurd. The press simply avoided the incomprehensible clause and thus we read: "Pilgrimages are not authorized," or "Pilgrimages have been forbidden." Pressure from certain highly placed sources contributed to this negative over-simplification.

Bishop Franić, Archbishop of Split and president of the Doctrinal Commission of the Yugoslav Bishops Conference, thus a person competent to make pronouncements in this regard, rectified these incomplete interpretations by issuing the following declaration:

"The Yugoslav Bishops did not intend to forbid all pilgrimages [....] Only those pilgrimages are forbidden which are led by pastors or the faithful who wish thereby to encroach upon the competent authority and/or anticipate its categorical and competent judgment.

"Pilgrims who go to Medjugorje in order to pray, to go to confession, to fast, and who do so in a spirit of submission to the definitive judgment to be made by the competent ecclesiastical authority, may do this with completely secure consciences according to the norms of Urban VIII confirmed by Paul VI (Code of Canon Law, 822-823)."

This declaration was issued by the Regina Pacis Society, a highly respected scientific, cultural and religious association, on the occasion of a journey by Bishop Franić to Rome. On that occasion, I also met with Bishop Franić as well as with the Holy Father to whom I presented copies of my two latest books on Medjugorje.